# SimplyEdu's Premier Prep for

## BY

*Neil Jeju and Noel Jeju*

ISBN: 979-8-321-60116-7

Any references to events, real people, or real places are used fictitiously. Names, characters, and places are products of the author's imagination.

AP® is a trademark owned by the College Board, which is not affiliated with, and does not endorse, this product.

Front Cover Design: Neil Jeju
Back Cover Design: Neil Jeju

First Print Edition 2024.

# TABLE OF CONTENTS

# Introduction

Congratulations for purchasing SimplyEdu's Premier Prep for AP® Precalculus! This book is designed to help students and teachers alike in learning the content of the course and becoming familiar with how to answer all types of questions successfully in order to be well prepared for the AP® exam. This book offers content explanations, practice problems, and 2 practice exams, along with explanations that cater to all types of learners. By going through this book, any student will be well prepared to achieve their desired score on the exam and have a strong base of knowledge and skills to prepare them well for future courses.

## How To Use This Book

## For Teachers

The multiple choice and free response strategies can be used to teach students effective methods on how to approach each question type. This knowledge is indispensable, as it helps students tackle question types more effectively. The content explanations in each module can be used to help explain or summarize content to the students. The unit 4 test is especially made to be used as an in-class test, though it can also be used to draw up questions to assign to students. Finally, the practice exams near the end of the book can be used near the end of the academic term to help gauge the students' overall learning and prepare them for the exam, though just like the practice problems it can also be used to draw up questions for in class assessments.

## For Students

This book can be used either for self-study or in conjunction with an in-school course. Regardless, most features in this book can be used the same way, although the timeline at which you are self-studying or reviewing may alter which features you choose to look over. The multiple choice and free response strategies can be useful in understanding how to attack certain types of questions. The content review sections are very helpful in explaining the information of the course. The practice problems at the end of each module can be used to review the content or prepare yourself for in-class assessments. The optional unit 4 test is especially helpful in this regard. Finally, the practice exams are very useful in testing oneself over the content and preparing for the official exam, though they can also be used to prepare for in-class assessments.

## AP® Exam Overview

The AP® Precalculus exam contains two main sections: multiple choice questions (MCQs) and free response questions (FRQs). There are a total of 40 multiple choice questions and 4 free response questions. Within the 40 multiple choice questions, 28 are to be done without a calculator, and time allotted for this section (section 1A) is 80 minutes. The remaining 12 questions require a graphing calculator, and the time allotted for this section (section 1B) is 40 minutes. Within the four free response questions, the first 2 (section IIA) require a graphing calculator and are meant to be done in 30 minutes. The remaining 2 (section IIB) are to be done without a calculator, and time allotted for this section is again 30 minutes. In terms of weight, section IA is responsible for 43.75% of the overall raw score, while sections IB, IIA, and IIB each account for 18.75% of the overall raw score. Unit 4, Functions involving parameters, vectors, and matrices, is not tested on the AP® Exam, but instead is offered as an additional unit, as the content within that unit is traditionally taught in precalculus courses. Thus, for students that plan to self-study the course, you should mainly focus on Units 1, 2, and 3. In terms of the weight of each unit on the AP® Exam, among the multiple-choice section, Unit 1 is weighted at 20-25%, Unit 2 is weighted at 22-28%, Unit 3 is weighted at 30-35%, and General Functions, a mixture of parts of Units 1 and 2, is responsible for 15-23%. The range of percentages is because the amount that each unit will show up on the exam fluctuates between each administration of the exam. By looking at these weights, it is clear that Unit 3 should receive a lot of focus. Within the free response section, questions 1 and 2 both focus on Units 1 and 2, while question 3 focuses on Unit 3, and question 4 focuses on Units 2 and 3. Questions 2 and 3 are in a real-world context, while questions 1 and 4 are not.

# Multiple Choice Question (MCQ) Strategies

As with all tests, it is vital to learn some test-taking tips ahead of time so that you can maximize your performance during the exam. First and foremost, read the question carefully. Often, many mistakes are made simply by not reading the question correctly and not seeing a negative sign, or not noticing that the word "not" was in the question. After that, try to solve the problem on your own and select the answer choice that you see most fit. However, if you are confused on the question or low on time, it often can be helpful to go straight to the answer choices. When evaluating answer choices, make sure to look through all the options and use process of elimination to remove wrong answers. To help with eliminating wrong answers, it is helpful to estimate what the correct answer might be, although this does not always apply. A very useful multiple-choice tip is to plug in the answer choices into the question. Again, this may not always apply, but when it does it is extremely helpful and can often save a lot of effort. Finally, pace yourself. As stated above, in section 1A you get 80 minutes to do 28 questions and in section 1B you get 40 minutes to do 12 questions, thus giving you a little under 3 minutes for 1A questions and 3 minutes 20 sections for 1B questions. It is important to watch your time as you take the test to ensure you are on pace, and it's highly recommended that you bubble in as you go, because it is likely that you will not be able to back later to look through all the questions and bubble in your answers onto the answer document. However, if you do have the time to go back, then use that time to first ensure that you correctly bubbled in your answer choices, and then go back once again to all the difficult questions to see if you may have a new insight that can lead you to the correct answer, if you have not already selected. As an extra tip, stay relaxed. Under periods of stress, one might not think at their best and overlook key details or information that could help to solve a question. Thus, it's important to stay relaxed. You got this!

# Free Response Question (FRQ) Strategies

When tackling the free-response section, the first step is to read all parts of the question. Often, answers to one part of a question are based on a previous answer, and thus reading all parts of the question can help serve as a guide to which way the problem should be approached. In order to earn all possible points, be sure to show all work neatly and in an organized manner when solving questions and include units on answers whenever applicable. Furthermore, make sure to allocate sufficient time for each part so that you can complete as many parts as possible. If a part or question seems too difficult, then skip it and save it for later. Additionally, practice very often, as not only will this help you to become accustomed to the different ways that certain question types should be approached, but also it helps train your hands to write out solutions under short periods of time. Also, use your calculator whenever allowed to, as this can help to save time. Finally, don't be stressed. You got this!

# Unit 1: Polynomial and Rational Functions

- Module 1: Rate of change

- Module 2: Polynomial Functions: Rates of Change, Complex Zeros, and End Behavior

- Module 3: Rational Functions: Zeros, Asymptotes, Holes, and End Behavior

- Module 4: Function Modeling

# Module 1: Rate of Change

A function is a mathematical relation in which every input value corresponds to exactly one output value. The set of input values, the independent variable, is the domain, while the set of output values, the dependent variable, is the range. The output values vary together—or in other words, in tandem—with the input values according to a function rule, which is an equation. For instance, $f(x) = 2x + 4$ is a function rule. You might see this rewritten as $y = 2x + 4$, as $y$ often represents as the output of a function. In the case of $f(x) = 2x + 4$, we have an increasing function, wherein as input values increase, output values also increase. For example, an input $x$-value of 2 results in an output $y$-value of 4. Increasing the input value to 4 causes the output value to increase to 12. On the other hand, for a function like $f(x) = -2x + 4$, an input value $x$-value of 2 results in an output $y$-value of 0, but increasing the $x$-value to 4 decreases the $y$-value to $-4$. This is an example of a decreasing function, because as input values increase, output values decrease. Some functions increase over certain parts of the function and decrease over other parts. In these cases, the function can be divided into increasing and decreasing intervals. For instance, consider the table for some of the values of the function $y = x^2$ below.

| $x$ | $-4$ | $-3$ | $-2$ | $-1$ | 0 | 1 | 2 | 3 | 4 |
|---|---|---|---|---|---|---|---|---|---|
| $y$ | 16 | 9 | 4 | 1 | 0 | 1 | 4 | 9 | 16 |

Of course, the $x$ and $y$ values for the function extend out to positive and negative infinity. When describing the increasing and decreasing intervals of the function, we say that the interval $(-\infty, 0)$ is decreasing, while the interval $(0, \infty)$ is increasing. The reason parentheses are used around positive and negative infinity is because the $x$-values don't truly reach positive or negative infinity, but rather approach those values. The reason that parentheses are used around the zeros is because at zero, the function is neither increasing nor decreasing, thus the value of 0 isn't a part of the interval but rather an endpoint, thus requiring parentheses. However, if we were to reduce the function down to just the x values from $-4$ to 4, then the interval $[-4,0)$ would be decreasing and $(0, 4]$ would be increasing. In this case, because $-4$ is a part of the decreasing interval, but not a turning point like 0, we use brackets around it to describe the interval. In general, when writing set notation, if a value is included in the set, brackets are used, and if it is not included in the set, parentheses are used. On the interval where the rate of change of a graph is increasing, the function is concave up, while on the interval where the rate of change of a graph is decreasing, we say the graph is concave down. A helpful way to understand how this appears on a graph is that on intervals where a function is concave up, it is shaped a cup (or at least a section of a cup), while on intervals where a function is concave down, it is shaped like a frown (or at least a section of a frown).

With these ideas of increasing and decreasing in mind, we can now introduce the idea of rate of change. Rate of change means exactly what the name implies: the rate at which a function changes over a given interval. Specifically, it is the rate of change in the output values in terms of the input values. This rate of change indicates how two quantities are associated, or in other words, how they vary together. In the previous equation, $y = x^2 + 4$, the $x$-values of 2 and 4 correspond to $y$-values are 8 and 20. To find our rate of change, we divide the change in output values by the change in input values. The specific formula and work for the given problem is below.

$$ROC = \frac{y_2 - y_1}{x_2 - x_1}$$

$$ROC = \frac{20 - 8}{4 - 2}$$

$$ROC = \frac{12}{2}$$

$$ROC = 6$$

If this formula and method looks familiar, it's because it should. What we just found is the slope of the secant line that intersects the graph at the points $(2,8)$ and $(4, 20)$. Our rate of change in this specific case is 6, which means that, over the interval [2,4], on average, every change in the x-values by 1 is associated with a change of 6 in the y-values, thus being an average rate of change. In this case, we have a positive rate of change. This means that an increase in $x$-values is associated with an increase in $y$-values. If we looked at the interval $[-4, -2]$, where the rate of change is $-6$, then it would be a negative rate of change.

For linear functions, such as $y = 2x + 4$, the rate of change throughout the function is constant. That is, for any given interval, let's say [1, 3] or [5, 7], the rate of change will be the same: 2. However, for quadratics, the rate of change changes linearly. This means that, for every equal interval of $x$-values, the rate of change will change by an amount that can be found linearly. For example, let's say you have the graph $y = x^2$. If we focus on the positive x axis, the $y$-value changes are as follows: 1, 3, 5, 7, 9, etc. This follows a linear pattern, and thus the rate of change for a quadratic is linear. For a better understanding on this topic, explore the idea of nth differences in module 4.

## Practice Problems
*A graphing calculator is permitted for all 3 of the following questions.*

1. Luke owns a store made to sell locally grown fruits and vegetables. The hourly sales for his store can be modeled by the function $y = -(x - 12)^2 + 510$, where $x$ is the hour on the 24-hour clock. What is the average rate of change in his sales from 2pm to 5pm?

    a. 17

    b. -7

    c. 12

    d. 4

2. Given the equation $f(x) = 3x^3 - 4x^2 - 8x - 1$, on which of the following intervals is the function strictly increasing?

   a. $[-2, -1]$

   b. $[1, 5]$

   c. $[0, 2]$

   d. $[2, 4]$

3. Given the function $f(x) = 7x + 2$, on which of the following intervals is the rate of change the highest?

   a. $[-1, 4]$

   b. $[2, 10]$

   c. $[3, 5]$

   d. The rate of change is the same for all the above intervals.

## Solutions

1. To find the average rate of change from 2pm to 5pm, we must take the $x$-values for 2pm and 5pm, plug them into the function to get their y values, and then use the slope formula to find the rate of change. Remember that x values are on the 24-hour clock. Thus, 2pm becomes 14 and 5pm becomes 17. Now, plugging in these two x values into the given function gives the values of 506 and 485, respectively. Plugging these into the slope formula gives us $-21/3$, simplifying down to a rate of change of $-7$. Thus, option B is the correct answer.

2. There are multiple ways to solve this question, such as looking at points within each interval to check for strict increasing. However, it is important to note that a graphing calculator is permitted for this question. Thus, simply type in the equation for the function and observe the graph on the calculator. This makes it much easier to see the proper interval. Among the answer choices, the only interval where $f(x)$ is strictly increasing is $[2, 4]$, and thus option D is the correct answer.

3. In this question, the function is linear, and thus the rate of change is constant throughout at 7, based on the coefficient of the $x$ term. Thus, option D is the correct answer.

# Module 2: Polynomial Functions: Rates of change, Complex Zeros, and End Behavior

Polynomial functions are any function defined by the formula $p(x) = a_n x^n + a_{n-1}x^{n-1} + a_{n-2}x^{n-2} + \cdots + a_2 x^2 + a_1 x + a_0 x^0$, where $n$ is a positive integer, and $a_i$ is a real number for each $i$ from 1 to $n$. A polynomial of degree $n$ has a leading term of $a_n x^n$. The rate of change of a polynomial function gets more complex as the degree of the polynomial gets larger. The two most basic forms of polynomial functions, constant and linear functions, have the simplest rates of change. A constant function defined as $y = c$ (this is still considered a polynomial function because it is seen as $cx^0$) has a rate of change of 0, because it has the same $y$-value for all values of $x$. Linear functions operate in a similar manner in that their rate of change is also constant. Linear functions are defined by the formula $y = ax + b$, and the rate of change of a linear function is the coefficient of $x$, $a$, and it is known as the slope. To prove this, you can take two points from the line and plug it into the formula below.

$$\frac{y_2 - y_1}{x_2 - x_1}$$

However, as we move on to polynomial functions of degree two or higher, the rates of change get more complex. This is because for any function of degree two or more, the rates of change changes between points. Let's take the quadratic function $f(x) = x^2 + 6x + 9$ as an example. The rate of change of the function at $x = 1$ is equal to 8, while the rate of change at $x = 2$ is equal to 10. In fact, for every single point on an infinitesimal level the rate of change is different.

Regardless, it is possible to find the average rate of change between two points on a nonlinear function using algebra. This average rate of change is equal to the slope of the secant line of the function on the given interval. The formula for this is:

$$\frac{f(b) - f(a)}{b - a}$$

Another way this formula could show up is in the form:

$$\frac{f(x + h) - f(x)}{h}$$

Both formulas are different forms of the slope formula. The first formula is essentially the same as the original slope formula with the $x_1$ and $x_2$ being exchanged for $a$ and $b$ respectively and $y_1$ and $y_2$ being exchanged for $f(a)$ and $f(b)$ respectively. The second formula can best be explained through its derivation.

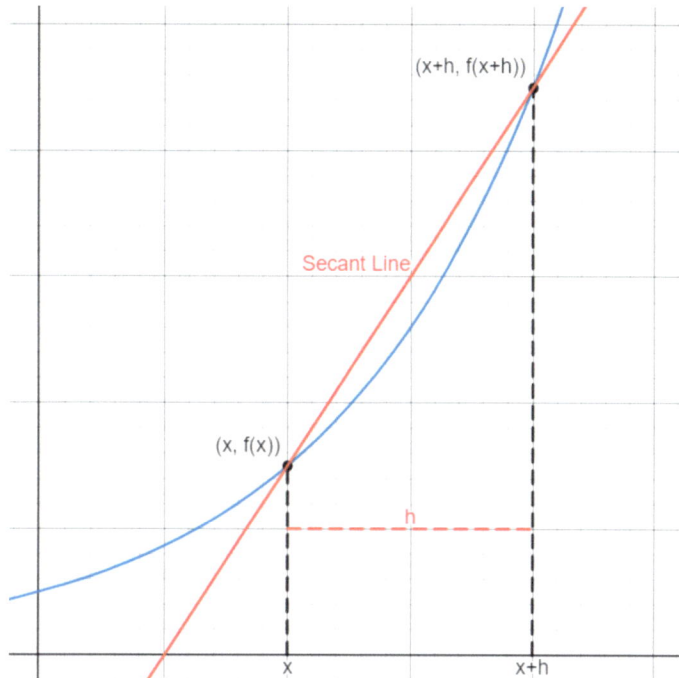

Figure 1(1). This graph was created on Desmos.com. The blue curve represents $f(x)$ and is of the function $y = \frac{3^x}{4}$. The secant line represents the average rate of change through the two points, which are labeled $(x, f(x))$ and $(x + h, f(x + h))$.

The first step to deriving this formula is to set up the slope formula. From the image we can get $f(x + h)$ as $y_2$, $f(x)$ as $y_2$, $x + h$ as $x_2$, and $x$ as $x_1$. Putting it all together we get:

$$\frac{f(x + h) - f(x)}{(x + h) - x}$$

If we remove the parentheses on the bottom, we can cancel out both $x$-terms, and we are left with:

$$\frac{f(x + h) - f(x)}{h}$$

If a polynomial function switches from increasing to decreasing over a given interval, the point at which this change occurs is known as a local/relative maximum. This is because relative to the points on its left and right side, the point is a maximum. Similarly, if a function switches from decreasing to increasing, it is known as a local/relative minimum. If a point has the highest $y$-value on a given interval, it is an absolute/global maximum, while the point with the lowest $y$-value on a given interval is the absolute/global minimum. Note that an absolute extremum doesn't have to be a relative extremum, as if an absolute extreme point is the endpoint of an interval, then there are no points on one of its sides to compare it to, and thus it cannot be called a relative extremum. For polynomial functions, a local extremum exists at least once between every two distinct real zeros. If a polynomial function is of even degree, then it must have either an absolute maximum or minimum, depending on the sign of the leading term. Points of inflection are where concavity changes.

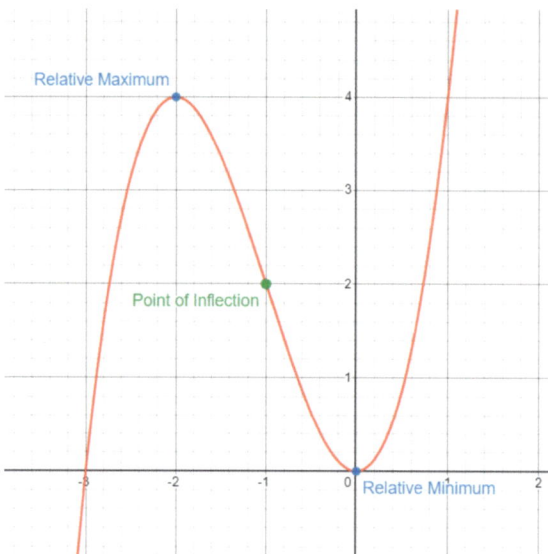

Figure 2 (1). This graph was made on desmos.com and is of the function $y = x^3 + 3x^2$. At the point $(-2, 4)$ there is a relative maximum, as that point has a y value higher than the points on its left and right sides. Similarly, a relative minimum is at $(0, 0)$. A point of inflection exists at $(-1, 2)$, as on the left of that point, the function is concave down (note the frown shape) while on the right of that point, the function is concave up (note the cup shape).

A zero of a polynomial function is located at points where the $y$-value of the function is 0, and thus a polynomial function has a zero at $x = c$ if $f(c) = 0$. If $c$ is a real number, then $(x - c)$ is a linear factor of the polynomial, and if $c$ is not a real number, then c is a complex zero of the function. Furthermore, if $c$ is a real zero of the function, then the graph of the polynomial has an $x$-intercept at $(c, 0)$. If these zeros are repeated, it is known as multiplicity. For instance, $y = (x - 1)^2$ has the zero $(1, 0)$ repeat twice, and thus this zero has a multiplicity of two. According to the Fundamental Theorem of Algebra, a polynomial function of degree $n$ has $n$ zeros, and these zeroes can have multiplicity larger than 1 and be complex. For instance, $y = (x - 1)^2$ has two zeros, both being $x = 1$. The multiplicity of a function at a given zero determines its behavior at that zero. If the multiplicity is even, the function bounces off the $x$-axis at that point, but if it is odd, then the function will pass through the $x$-axis. Finally, if a polynomial function has the complex zero $a + bi$ , then it must also have the complex zero $a - bi$. For instance, the function $f(x) = x^3 + 8$. This factors down into $(x + 2)(x^2 - 2x + 4)$, resulting in the zeros of $x = -2, 1 + i\sqrt{3}, 1 - i\sqrt{3}$.

Specific functions are classified as even or odd functions. An odd function is of the form $f(x) = a_n x^n$, where $n$ is an odd integer greater than or equal to 1. These functions have the property of being symmetric about the origin and $f(-x) = -f(x)$. An interesting property is that the sum of odd functions is another odd function, and thus $f(x) = x^7 + x^5 + x^3 + x$ is odd.

Even functions are in the form $f(x) = a_n x^n$, where n is an even integer larger than 1. Graphically, these are symmetric over the y-axis, and have the property $f(-x) = f(x)$. Once again, the sum of even functions is an even function, and thus $f(x) = x^8 + x^6 + x^4 + x^2 + 2$ is even.

The end behavior of a function is the value that the function approaches as $x$ approaches positive or negative infinity. For polynomials, the end behavior is based off the leading term. This is because as the $x$-values approach the extremes, the terms with the highest power dominate the values of the lower power terms. For functions where the leading term has an even power, the left and right end behavior is the same, while they are opposites for functions with an odd power on the leading term. Furthermore, for both functions, if the leading term has a negative sign, then as the $x$-values approach infinity, the $y$-values approach negative infinity. For functions with a positive coefficient and even power on the leading term, this is the corresponding mathematical notation for end behavior: $\lim_{x \to \infty} f(x) = \infty$ and $\lim_{x \to -\infty} f(x) = \infty$. For functions with a negative coefficient and odd power on the leading term, the end behavior in limit notation is $\lim_{x \to \infty} f(x) = -\infty$ and $\lim_{x \to -\infty} f(x) = \infty$.

## Practice Problems

*A graphing calculator is permitted for all 3 of the following questions.*

1. A polynomial function $f$ is given by $f(x) = 6x^4 - 3x^2 + 2x^7$. Which of the following statements about the end behavior of $f$ is true?

    a. The sign of the leading term of $f$ is positive, and the degree of the leading term of $f$ is odd; thus, $\lim_{x \to -\infty} f(x) = -\infty$ & $\lim_{x \to \infty} f(x) = \infty$

    b. The sign of the leading term of $f$ is positive, and the degree of the leading term of $f$ is even; thus, $\lim_{x \to -\infty} f(x) = \infty$ & $\lim_{x \to \infty} f(x) = \infty$

    c. The sign of the leading term of $f$ is negative, and the degree of the leading term of $f$ is odd; thus, $\lim_{x \to -\infty} f(x) = \infty$ & $\lim_{x \to \infty} f(x) = -\infty$

    d. The sign of the leading term of $f$ is negative, and the degree of the leading term of $f$ is even; thus, $\lim_{x \to -\infty} f(x) = -\infty$ & $\lim_{x \to \infty} f(x) = -\infty$

2. A polynomial function $f$ is an even function where $f(7) = 2$ is a local minimum. Which of the following statements about $f(-7)$ must be true?

    a. $f(-7) = 2$ is a local maximum.

    b. $f(-7) = 2$ is a local minimum.

    c. $f(-7) = -2$ is a local maximum.

    d. $f(-7) = -2$ is a local minimum.

3. The polynomial function $f$ is defined $f(x) = 4(x - 1)^2(x + 2)^3(x^2 + 2x + 4)$. Which of the following is true for $f(x)$?

a. $x = 1$ is a zero with a multiplicity of 3.

b. $x = -2$ is a zero with a multiplicity of 2.

c. $f(x)$ has one non-real zero.

d. $f(x)$ has 7 total zeros.

## Solutions

1. In this question, we are asked to find the end behavior of the given function. To do that, we must first identify the leading term, which is not $6x^4$ but rather $2x^7$. Based on this, the leading term has a positive coefficient and odd power. Therefore, option A is the correct answer choice.

2. In this question, we are asked to determine a property of a point on an even function. Even functions have the identity that $f(-x) = f(x)$, and thus local extrema remain the same across the y axis. Therefore, the point $(7, 2)$ corresponds with $(-7, 2)$, and because $(7, 2)$ is a local minimum, $(-7, 2)$ must also be a local minimum. Therefore, option B is the correct answer choice.

3. In this question, we are asked to find a property of $f(x)$ given the factored equation. Because $(x - 1)$ has a power of 2, $x = 1$ is a zero with multiplicity of 2, so eliminate option A. For similar reasons, eliminate option B. The quadratic factor of $(x^2 + 2x + 4)$ yields two non-real zeros, and if you remember earlier, every complex zero has its conjugate partner also as zero. Eliminate option C. By all the powers of x to find the leading term, you yield 7, and according to the Fundamental Theorem of Algebra, this function must have 7 roots. Thus, option D is the correct answer choice.

# Module 3: Rational Functions: End Behavior, Discontinuities, and Polynomial Division

To continue our discussion of functions, our next stop is rational functions, which are essentially polynomials with division. For example, observe $f(x)$ below.

$$f(x) = \frac{x^2 - 1}{x + 1}$$

This is a quadratic function divided by a linear function. Because of how important division is in reference to rational functions, it's the first concept that we need to understand. To do this, we need to discuss our method of polynomial division: long division. We set this up in the same way that we would do numeric long division, with $x^2 - 1$ as our dividend and $x + 1$ as our divisor. However, when writing in $x^2 - 1$, and in general whenever you write out an expression to be divided through long division, it is important to first scan for missing terms, that being to look for if you are missing any power of the variable that is less than that of the leading term. In this case, we do not have a linear term (a term where the power of $x$ is 1), so we write in $+0x$ to account for this.

$$x+1\overline{)\,x^2 + 0x - 1}$$

To divide, we compare the leading terms, which is the term with the largest exponent, of both the dividend and divisor. In this case, we have $x^2$ and $x$, so we would divide $x^2$ by $x$ to get $x$, and put that into our quotient, and then multiply it by the divisor to subtract it from the dividend, as we would in numeric long division. In this case, multiplying $x$ by $x + 1$ gives us $x^2 + x$, so we would subtract that from our dividend.

$$
\begin{array}{r}
x \phantom{xxxxxx} \\
x+1\overline{)\,x^2 + 0x - 1} \\
\underline{-(x^2 + x)\phantom{xx}} \\
-x - 1
\end{array}
$$

After this, we must again divide until we get to a point where the highest power of the remainder is lower than that of the divisor, so in our case we must have a constant as our remainder, as our leading term of the divisor is linear. To divide again, we divide $-x$ by $x$ to get $-1$, which we put into our quotient, and then multiply $-1$ by $x+1$ to get $-x-1$ and subtract that from the $-x-1$ in the previous division. The result of this subtraction should be our remainder.

$$
\begin{array}{r}
x - 1 \phantom{xxx} \\
x + 1\overline{)\,x^2 + 0x - 1} \\
\underline{-x^2 - x\phantom{xxxx}} \\
-x - 1 \\
\underline{-(-x - 1)} \\
0
\end{array}
$$

Thus, our quotient is $x - 1$ and our remainder is 0. Let's do another example: $(x^3 - x + 7) \div (x - 4)$. Just as before, we must first look for if we are missing any terms, and this case we are missing a quadratic term, so we must add in $+0x^2$ when writing out the expression. After that, we divide the same way we did in the previous problem.

$$x^2 + 4x + 15 + \frac{67}{x-4}$$

$$\begin{array}{r} x\text{-}4 \overline{) x^3 + 0x^2 - x + 7} \\ \underline{-(x^3 - 4x^2)} \\ 4x^2 - x \\ \underline{-(4x^2 - 16x)} \\ 15x + 7 \\ \underline{-(15x - 60)} \\ 67 \end{array}$$

Thus, our quotient is $x^2 + 4x + 15$, and our remainder is $\frac{67}{x-4}$. Note that all we must do for our remainder is get the final resultant, in this case 67, and then make it a fraction with the numerator being the resultant and the denominator being the divisor of the initial problem.

Now that we got division out of the way, we can begin to talk about the end behavior of polynomials and later rational functions. To start, we must first discuss what end behavior is. End behavior is the value that the function approaches as the $x$-values approach negative and positive infinity. To determine this, we must first focus on leading terms. As stated before, a leading term is the term in a polynomial with the largest exponent. In the previous problem, the leading term of the dividend was $x^3$, as that is the term with the largest exponent on the $x$-variable. For polynomial functions, there are two main considerations that must be made in order to describe the end behavior: the exponent of the leading term and the sign. For a given polynomial, if the exponent of the leading term is even, then the end behavior will be the same on both sides of the polynomial, meaning that the value that the polynomial approaches as the $x$-values approach negative infinity will be the same value that the polynomial approaches as the $x$-values approach positive infinity. For the sign, a positive leading term means that as the $x$-values approach positive infinity, the $y$-values approach positive infinity, and if the leading term has a negative coefficient, then as the $x$-values approach positive infinity, the $y$-values approach negative infinity. Combining these two ideas together, we can figure out the end behavior for all basic polynomials.

| | Positive Coefficient | Negative Coefficient |
|---|---|---|
| Odd Exponent | As $x$ approaches negative infinity, $y$ approaches negative infinity. As $x$ approaches positive infinity, $y$ approaches positive infinity. | As $x$ approaches negative infinity, $y$ approaches positive infinity. As $x$ approaches positive infinity, $y$ approaches negative infinity. |
| Even Exponent | As $x$ approaches negative infinity or positive infinity, $y$ approaches positive infinity. | As $x$ approaches negative infinity or positive infinity, $y$ approaches negative infinity. |

Suppose we had the function $f(x) = -x^3$. The leading term has a negative coefficient and an odd power, so we know that as x approaches negative infinity, $y$ approaches positive infinity, and as $x$ approaches positive infinity, $y$ approaches negative infinity. The specific mathematical notation for this is as follows:

$$\lim_{x \to \infty} f(x) = -\infty \text{ and } \lim_{x \to -\infty} f(x) = \infty$$

The way that this would be read is "the limit of $f$ of $x$ as $x$ approaches infinity is negative infinity, and the limit of $f$ of $x$ as $x$ approaches negative infinity is infinity". Let's do another example. $f(x) = x^4 - 2x^3 - 3x^5 - 5x + 2$. The end behavior is as $x$ approaches negative infinity, $y$ approaches positive infinity and as $x$ approaches positive infinity, $y$ approaches positive infinity right? Wrong. The leading term is not $x^4$ but rather $-3x^5$, and thus the actual leading behavior is as $x$ approaches negative infinity, $y$ approaches positive infinity, and as $x$ approaches positive infinity, $y$ approaches negative infinity. In limit notation, it would be written as follows:

$$\lim_{x \to \infty} f(x) = -\infty \text{ and } \lim_{x \to -\infty} f(x) = \infty$$

Next up is the end behavior of rational functions. This can be found through combining the function that results from dividing the numerator and denominator and adding the discontinuities onto it. Discontinuities are places in a function where the graph loses its connection. These come in the form of holes and asymptotes. Holes are, as the name implies, a specific point where the function does not exist and thus doesn't have a point there. In certain cases, a given $x$ value may have a point and a hole, such as in step functions, and this would still be considered discontinuity as the function is no longer continuous.

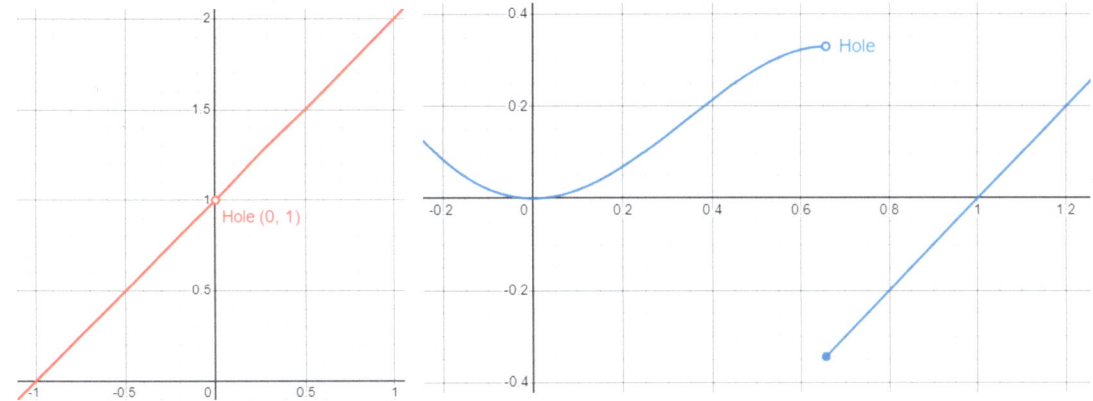

Figures 3 and 4 (1). The graphs above were made on Desmos.com. The graph on the left is of the function $y = \frac{x(x+1)}{x}$ and has a hole at (0, 1). The graph on the right is a piecewise function of a quintic function and a line, and the quintic function ends on a hole where at the same x value, the line begins.

Holes form through the presence of both zero in the numerator and denominator of a given function. Suppose $f(x) = \frac{(x+1)(x-2)}{(x+1)}$. At the $x$-value of $-1$, both the numerator and the denominator will be equal to 0 due to the $x + 1$ factor in both parts of the fraction. To find the $y$ value of this hole, divide out the $x + 1$ from both the numerator and denominator, and plug in the $x$-value of $-1$ to the remaining function. So, we plug in $x = -1$ into $x - 2$, giving us $-3$. Thus, there is a hole at the point $(-1, -3)$. For functions like the line shown on the left, it is often possible to approximate the y value where the hole will be. In these cases, we can say that as the $x$-values approach the $x$-value of where the hole is, the $y$ values approach the $y$-value of where the hole should be. Assuming a hole with coordinates $(a, b)$, we can write this in limit notation as the following.

$$\lim_{x \to a} f(x) = b$$

Also, it is important to note that the function should reach the value $b$ regardless of which direction you approach $a$, meaning regardless of if you approach $a$ from the left side or the right side, you should still approach $b$. Thus, we can also write the limit notation as follows, where the first indicates approaching a from the left side and the second indicates approaching a from the right side.

$$\lim_{x \to a^-} f(x) = b \qquad\qquad \lim_{x \to a^+} f(x) = b$$

The other type of discontinuity is an asymptote. These are lines that the function approaches but doesn't (usually) touch. The three types of asymptotes are horizontal asymptotes, vertical asymptotes, and slant asymptotes. Functions may cross slant or horizontal asymptotes, but never cross vertical asymptotes.

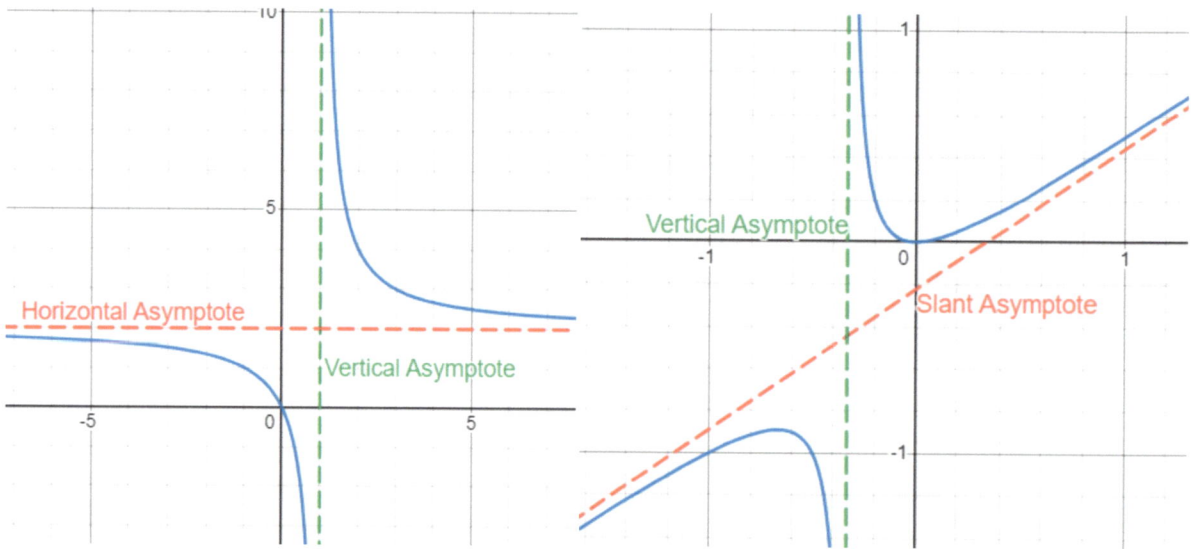

Figure 5 and 6 (1). The graphs above were made on Desmos.com. In the graph on the left, a vertical asymptote exists at $x = 1$, and the function approaches the vertical asymptote from both the left and right side, but do not intersect it. The same applies for the vertical asymptote on the graph on the right. In the graph on the left, a horizontal asymptote exists at $y = 2$, while in the graph on the right, a slant asymptote exists with the equation $y = \frac{2}{3}x - \frac{2}{9}$. In both cases, the function approaches the values of the asymptote.

The way that vertical asymptotes form is when there is a 0 in just the denominator. As we know, you cannot divide by 0, as that is undefined, and thus the function does not cross this $x$ value. At these $x$ values, the function increases and decreases to approach positive and negative infinity based on the direction that you look at the $x$ values. For example, in figure 5, there's a vertical asymptote at $x = 1$. As you approach the vertical asymptote from the left side, and thus the negative values of $x$, the $y$ values approach negative infinity, while approaching the asymptote when you start at the right side results in $y$ values approaching positive infinity. In limit notation, it would be written as follows:

$$\lim_{x \to 0^-} f(x) = -\infty \qquad\qquad \lim_{x \to 0^+} f(x) = \infty$$

There are two cases that form horizontal asymptotes. The first is when the exponent of the leading term of the denominator is larger than that of the numerator. In this case, as the $x$ values approach the extremes, the values of the denominator will be significantly larger than those of the numerator, and thus we get a horizontal asymptote at the line $y = 0$. The other case that forms horizontal asymptotes is when the exponents of the leading terms of the numerator and the denominator are equal. In this case, we divide the coefficients of the leading terms to find the horizontal asymptotes. This makes sense, because as the $x$ values approach the extremes, it's the leading terms that become the most important and the largest in magnitude, and thus if the leading terms have the same exponent, we can ignore the remaining terms in the numerator and denominator and divide out the variable part of the leading term to find what our horizontal asymptote is. Thus, for $y = \frac{2x^2 - 3}{4x^2}$, the horizontal asymptote is $y = \frac{1}{2}$.

The final type of asymptote is formed when the exponent of the leading term of the numerator is larger than that of the denominator. In this case, there is no horizontal asymptote. However, if the exponent of the leading term is larger than that of the denominator by 1, there is a slant asymptote, which is when a line is the asymptote. This is found by dividing the numerator by the denominator and disregarding the remainder. An example would be $y = 2x - 1$ for the function $f(x) = \frac{2x^2 - x + 3}{x}$.

All of the above may be difficult to remember at first, but there is a very easy acronym to help with that: Bob0 Botn Eats dc. The Bob0 stands for bigger on bottom, 0. This means that if the exponent of the leading term of the denominator (bottom) is bigger than that of the numerator, you have a horizontal asymptote at $y = 0$. The botn stands for bigger on top, none. This means if the exponent of the leading term of the numerator is bigger than that of the denominator, then there is no horizontal asymptote, but instead a slant asymptote. Finally, the eats dc stands for exponents are the same, divide coefficients. This means that if the exponents of the leading terms of the numerator and the denominator are the same, then simply divide the coefficients of the leading terms to find the horizontal asymptote.

The final topic to cover is zeros. The zeros of a rational function are found by finding the zeros of the polynomial function in the numerator of the rational function. However, these are only zeros of the rational function if they are not zeros of the denominator. Zeros of the denominator result in the discontinuities discussed above. Thus, for the function $f(x) = \frac{x^2 - 1}{x + 1}$, the numerator has the zeros of 1 and $-1$ while the denominator has a zero of $-1$. Thus, we have a hole at the $x$ value of $-1$ and a zero at the $x$ value of 1.

## Practice Problems

*All 3 of the following questions are to be done without the use of a calculator*

1. Jacob was studying film over his favorite basketball player's highlights and noticed that the arc of the player's jump shot can be approximated by the function $f(x) = -0.25x^4 + 0.5x^3 + x^2 + 2$. He then graphed this function and allowed it to extend infinitely. Which of the following gives the correct limit notation for the end behavior of the function?

   a. $\lim\limits_{x \to -\infty} f(x) = \infty$ and $\lim\limits_{x \to \infty} f(x) = \infty$

b. $\lim\limits_{x \to -\infty} f(x) = -\infty$ and $\lim\limits_{x \to \infty} f(x) = \infty$

c. $\lim\limits_{x \to -\infty} f(x) = \infty$ and $\lim\limits_{x \to \infty} f(x) = -\infty$

d. $\lim\limits_{x \to -\infty} f(x) = -\infty$ and $\lim\limits_{x \to \infty} f(x) = -\infty$

2. Consider the rational function $f(x) = \frac{x^2 - 4}{x - 2}$ is given. Which of the following is true about the zeros of this function?

    a. The function has two zeros at $x = -2$ and $x = 2$

    b. The function has one zero at $x = -2$

    c. The function has no real zeros but two complex zeros.

    d. The function has no zeros.

3. A rational function is defined as $f(x) = \frac{3x^2 + 2x - 1}{x^2 - 9}$. Which of the following statements correctly describes the vertical asymptotes of this function?

    a. There are vertical asymptotes at $x = -3$ and $x = 3$

    b. There is a vertical asymptote at $x = 3$

    c. There is a vertical asymptote at $x = -3$

    d. There are no vertical asymptotes.

## Solutions

1. In this problem, we are asked to find the end behavior of the function, and thus we must focus on the leading term, which is $-0.25x^4$. We have a negative coefficient and an even power. Thus, we know that as x approaches both positive and negative infinity, f(x) approaches negative infinity. Thus, the correct answer choice is option D.

2. In this problem, we are asked to find the zeros of the function. Thus, we must find the zeros of the numerator and see if they align with those of the denominator. The numerator can be factored out into $(x + 2)(x - 2)$. Thus, the zeros of the numerator are $-2$ and 2. From there, we must look at the zero of the denominator, which is 2. Because 2 appears as a zero of both the numerator and the denominator, we cannot consider it a zero of the function (rather, a hole exists at this point). Therefore, the zero of the function is $-2$, so answer choice B is correct.

3. In this problem, we are asked to find the vertical asymptotes of the function. Thus, we should factor out the numerator and denominator, and all the zeros of the denominator but not the numerator constitute our vertical asymptotes. Our numerator can be factored out to $(3x - 1)(x + 1)$ while our denominator can be factored out to $(x - 3)(x + 3)$. Because none of our factors overlap, the zeros of the denominator are the vertical asymptotes of the function. Thus, we have vertical asymptotes at $x = 3$ and $x = -3$, so the correct answer choice is option A.

# Module 4: Function Modeling and Transformations

To start off this chapter, we begin with function transformations. There are essentially two types of transformations: shifts and dilations, which are also called additive and multiplicative transformations respectively. First let's focus on the shifts. There are two types of shifts: horizontal shifts and vertical shifts. To describe a shift, let's suppose we have an initial function $f(x)$ and our transformed function $g(x)$. Vertical shifts are in the form $g(x) = f(x) + k$, where $k$ is some positive or negative constant. If $k$ is positive, then the entire function is shifted up by $k$ units, and if $k$ is negative, the function goes down by $k$ units. This makes sense, as we're literally adding or subtracting $k$ to every y value, so every y value changes by $k$ units. Horizontal transformations are in the form $g(x) = f(x + h)$, where a positive $h$ means the function is shifted left by $h$ units and a negative $h$ means the function is shifted right by $h$ units. To understand why it causes a shift left, imagine $h = 2$. Now, $g(x) = f(x + 2)$, meaning $g(0) = f(2)$, $g(1) = f(3)$, etc. As a result, $g(x)$ will have the same y-values of $f(x)$ but 2 x-values earlier, indicating a shift *left* by 2.

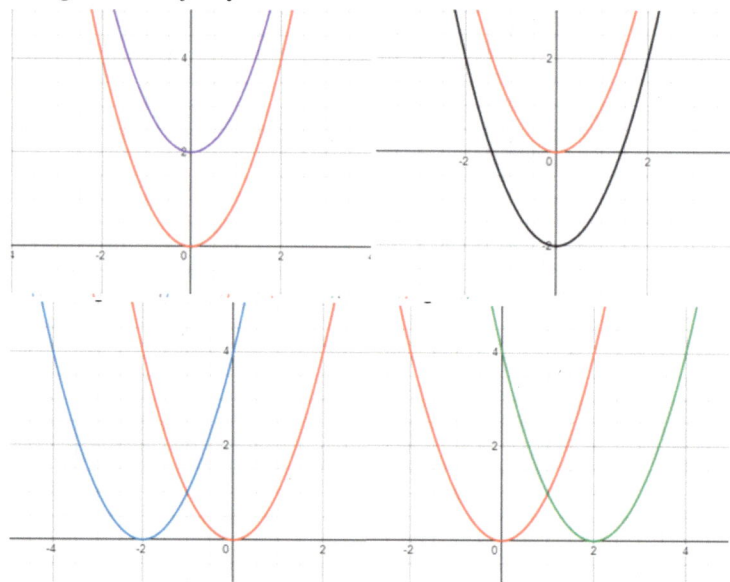

Figure 7 (1). The images above are taken from graphs made using Desmos.com. All graphs include y=x², with the top left showing a shift up, the top right a shift down, the bottom left a shift left, and the bottom right a shift right.

Next are the multiplicative transformations, also called dilations. In this case, the transformations can either be vertical or horizontal dilations. Vertical dilations are in the form $g(x) = af(x)$, where $a \neq 0$. The function is stretched vertically by $|a|$, and if $a$ is negative, then the function is reflected over the x axis. For instance, if we have $f(x) = x^2$, and then $g(x) = 2f(x)$, then instead of the point (1,1) in $f(x)$, $g(x)$ would have (1,2), and instead of (2,4), it will have (2,8). The horizontal dilations are in the form $g(x) = f(bx)$, where $b \neq 0$. The function is stretched horizontally by $\left|\frac{1}{b}\right|$, and if b is negative then the function is reflected over the y axis. To stretch horizontally by a fraction simply means to condense the graph by that amount. For instance, for $f(x) = x^2$ and $g(x) = f(2x)$, instead of (1,1), $g(x)$ has (0.5, 1) and instead of (2,4), $g(x)$ has (1,4), and thus note that every $x$-value of $f$ got multiplied by $\frac{1}{2}$ while the $y$-values were kept the same. If this is confusing, remember that by doing $f(2x)$, an input of $x$ gets the $y$-value that corresponds to $2x$, and thus you can think about it as that the graph is reaching $y$-values earlier (in the positive section of the $x$ axis) than it normally does, thus meaning that the graph is condensed.

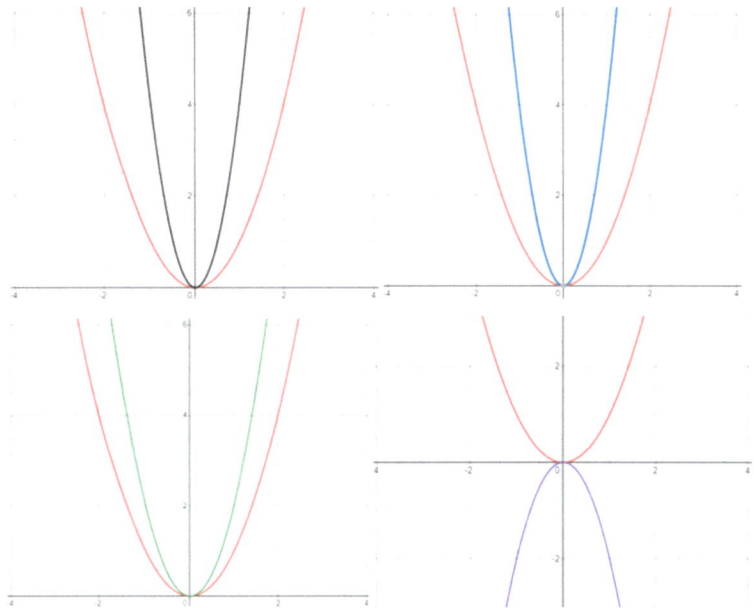

Figure 8 (1). The images above are taken from graphs made using Desmos.com. All graphs include $y = x^2$, with the top left showing a horizontal stretch by 2, the top right a reflection across the y axis and a horizontal stretch by 2, the bottom vertical stretch by 2, and the bottom right a reflection across the x axis and a vertical stretch by 2.

Thus, we have 4 basic transformations: vertical shifts, horizontal shifts, vertical dilations, and horizontal dilations. Note that any combination of them can be done to produce a new function. Also, with this idea of transformations in mind, we can think of any function as a transformed version of the parent function, and thus we can calculate the domain and range of these functions by using the domain and range of the parent and then applying the appropriate transformations.

Next, we need to discuss using the right function for a given scenario. It is known that linear functions are those with constant rates of change, so scenarios where the rate of change is constant usually follow a linear model. In a similar way, because quadratic functions are those with linear rates of change, scenarios that have a linearly changing rate of change follow a quadratic model. Note that quadratic models also apply to scenarios that involve symmetric data and a minimum or maximum, based on the situation. Using this idea of rate of change, functions of area (two dimensions), can be modeled by quadratic functions, while contexts of volume (three dimensions) use cubic functions. For instance, if we have a rectangle in which the side lengths are 4 and 6, and we want to see what the area will be every time we increase the side lengths by the same amount, we can set one side as $x$ and another as $x + 2$, and thus have the function $a(x) = x^2 + 2x$, where x is the length of the shorter side and $a(x)$ is the area of the rectangle. If the data is inversely proportional, such as speed in relation to time or gravity in relationship to distance, then a rational function is the most appropriate for the data.

As for choosing a function based on the number of points given, a function with degree $n$ or less can model a graph with $n + 1$ points. For instance, if given three points, either a quadratic function or a linear function to model the data, based on what fits better. However, if you are given multiple coordinate points, or even a data table, and know for sure that it follows a function, then there is a surefire method to find the degree of the polynomial: $n$th differences. Let's look at a data table to understand this better.

| $x$ | 1 | 2 | 3 | 4 | 5 |
|------|---|---|----|----|----|
| $f(x)$ | 3 | 9 | 19 | 33 | 51 |

To find when we have constant differences, we must repeatedly subtract the $y$-values, and the number of times it takes to get constant differences is the degree of the polynomial. Here's what that looks like.

| $x$ intervals | 1-2 | 2-3 | 3-4 | 4-5 |
|------|------|------|------|------|
| $f(x)$ difference $(d_1)$ | (3-9) = -6 | (9-19) = -10 | (19-33) = -14 | (33-51) = -18 |
| $d_2$ | (-6- -10) = 4 | (-10- -14) = 4 | (-14- -18) = 4 | |

Thus, at the $2^{nd}$ difference, we got a constant difference of 4, and thus we know that this data follows a quadratic function, which in fact it does. These values are from the function $f(x) = 2x^2 + 1$.

The above situations all describe cases in which the data is able fully follow just one model. However, this is not always the case, as often some functions have certain intervals where they follow one model, and other intervals a different one. This is where piecewise-defined functions come in. A piecewise-defined function, often called a piecewise function, is one that contains multiple functions over nonoverlapping $x$ intervals, and thus they often have holes at the beginning or end of each piece. Here's an example:

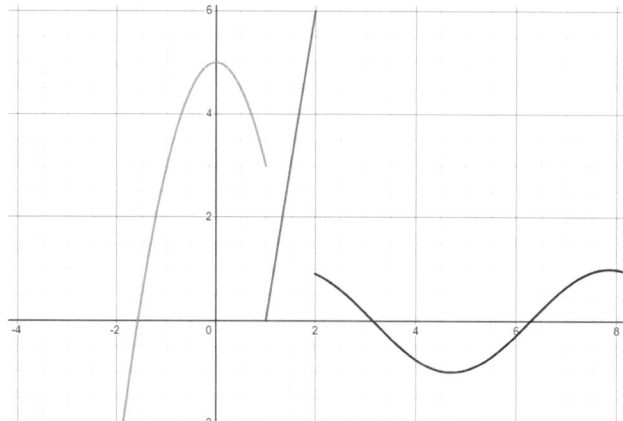

Figure 9 (1). The image above is from a graph made on Desmos.com. The piecewise function contains 3 parts, the leftmost part being $y = -2x^2 + 5$, the middle being $y = 6x - 6$, and the right being $y = \sin x$. Notice how the different pieces of the graph do not overlap and have their own x interval.

## Practice Problems

*All 3 of the following questions are to be done without the use of a calculator*

1. Consider the parent quadratic function $f(x) = x^2$. Which of the following transformations create the function $g(x) = -(x - 3)^2 + 4$?

a. A vertical stretch by a factor of 2, a horizontal translation 3 units to the right, and a vertical translation 4 units up

b. A reflection across the x axis, a horizontal translation 3 units to the left, and a vertical translation 4 units up

c. A reflection across the x axis, a horizontal translation 3 units to the right, and a vertical translation 4 units up

d. A reflection across the x axis, a horizontal translation 4 units to the left, and a vertical translation 3 units up

2. A sequence of numbers is given as 3, 7, 13, 21, … . Which of the following functions $f(n)$ correctly gives the nth term of the sequence? Use the constant nth difference to help pinpoint your answer.

   a. $f(n) = 2n^2 - 3n + 1$

   b. $f(n) = n^2 + n + 1$

   c. $f(n) = n + 4$

   d. $f(n) = 2n + 3$

3. Given the following piecewise-defined function, which of the following is true about $f(x)$?

$$f(x) = \begin{cases} 2x + 3 \ for \ x \leq 1 \\ x^2 + 1 \ for \ x > 1 \end{cases}$$

   a. At $x = 1$, the function has an infinite discontinuity

   b. At $x = 1$, the function has a jump discontinuity

   c. At $x = 1$, the y value is 2

   d. At $x = 1$, the y value is 3.5

## Solutions

1. When analyzing this function, we notice a negative sign in front of the x portion of the function, meaning that there is a reflection across the x axis. Thus, we must eliminate option a. After that, there is a -3, meaning a horizontal shift 3 units to the right. Thus, we must eliminate options b and d, meaning c is the only correct choice. However, to confirm, there is a plus 4 at the end of the function, meaning a vertical translation 4 units up, confirming c to the be the correct answer choice.

2. Using the constant nth difference, we see that the 2nd difference is constant at a value of 2, meaning we have a quadratic function, allowing us to eliminate

options c and d. From there, we can test out n is 1 for the value 3. Plugging in 1 into the first function gets us 0, but plugging in 1 for the second function gives us 3. Thus, b is the correct answer choice. To confirm, we can use subsequent n values and compare them to the sequence.

3. In this piecewise-defined function, it appears that the first piece ends at the x value of 1 and the next piece starts immediately after 1. Plugging in $x = 1$ to the two pieces yields 5 and 2, indicating that the function is not continuous at $x = 1$, but because a point does exist, the function is "jumping" from one piece to another, indicating a jump discontinuity. Furthermore, because $x = 1$ is a part of the first piece, and not the second, the y value for $x = 1$ is 5, eliminating choices c and d. This leads us to answer choice b. To confirm if we are correct, substitute $x = 1$ for the first piece of the function. This gives us 5, which is not either of the answer choices. Thus, b is the correct answer choice.

# Unit 2: Exponential and Logarithmic Functions

- Module 5: Function Validation and Composition

- Module 6: Changes in Sequences and Functions

- Module 7: Exponential Functions

- Module 8: Logarithmic Functions

# Module 5: Function Validation and Composition

      The first module of this new unit is on function validation and composition. Validation of a function is determining whether the model that we used is the most appropriate for a given data set. For a given data set, we can use many types of models to show what function the data is most like: a line, a parabola, or even an exponential or logarithmic curve. Usually, we determine the type of model most fit for the data either by directly looking at it or using context clues based on what situation the data is modeling. The way that we guarantee that the model we used is appropriate is through the residual plot. For a given model, the residuals are the difference between the actual value given in the data set versus the expected value that is predicted by the function. For instance, suppose the function $f(x) = 2x + 3$ and the data point $(2, 10)$. To find what the expected value is, we plug in the x-value of 2 to see what the function says the y-value should be. By plugging it in, we see that $f(2)$ is 7. However, the data point given had a y-value of 10. To find our residual, we subtract 7 from 10 to get 3, so our residual is 3. Here is a look at a graph and some of its residuals.

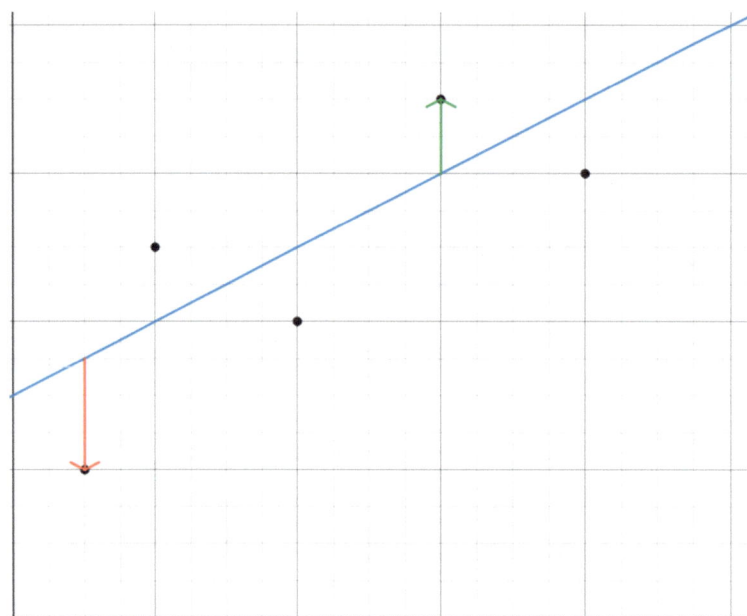

Figure 10 (1). The graph above was made on Desmos.com. The blue line represents the line of best fit through the given points. The red arrow from the line of best fit to a data point and the green arrow from the line of best fit to another point represent the residual, which is the difference between the expected value by the line of best fit for a given x value and the actual value of the point

      After taking the residuals of all the points, we can then plot the residuals on a graph where the center of the y axis is on 0. An example is shown in figure 11. If the model we used is the most appropriate, then there should be no recognizable pattern in the residual plot. If there is no pattern, then we can attribute the differences between the expected and actual values to be due to chance, or maybe some small underlying event that occurred for one data measurement only. However, if there is a pattern, then that means we must change our model. If the pattern is the same type of function of the one that we already used, then we simply need to alter the coefficients. However, if it is a different type of function, then we must use a different model. Finally, the error is the overall difference between predicted and actual values is the error.

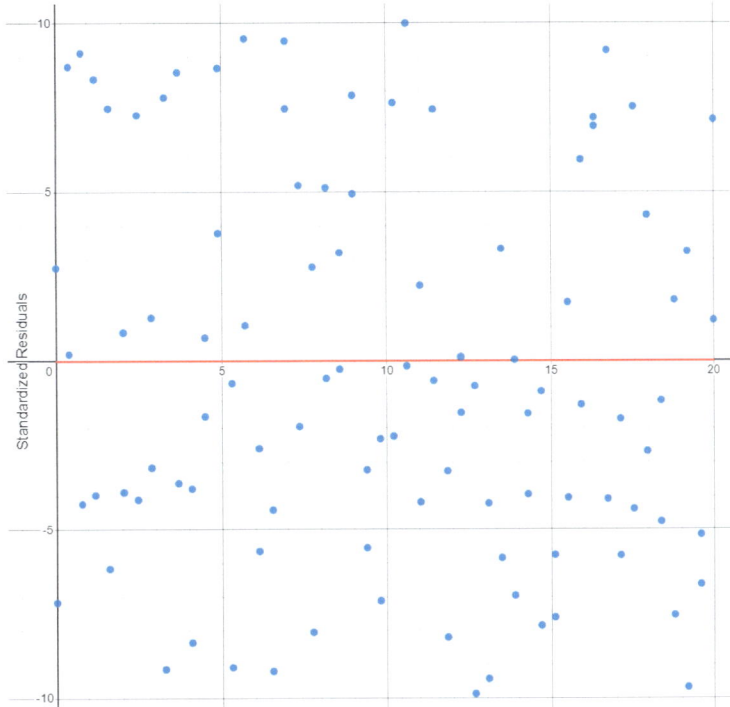

Figure 11 (1). This residual plot was made on Desmos.com. The red line is at 0, which would represent a point that lied exactly on the line of best fit. The 100 blue data points all represent the residuals of 100 points, with the residuals ranging from -10 to positive 10. Notice, no clear pattern exists with the residuals, and thus it can be said that the model used to create this residual plot was effective.

Next up we have composition of functions. A composition of functions is when the range of one function is used as the domain for another function. It can be written as $f(g(x))$ or $(f \circ g)(x)$ . An easy way to think of this is that you do the function twice: first you use the actual $x$-values to plug in to $g(x)$, thus giving you the y values of $g(x)$. Then you plug in these $y$-values into $f(x)$, and basically treat these $y$-values as if they were $x$-values. The resulting $f(g(x))$ values are the range of the composition, while the domain was the initial $x$-values plugged in. When you do this, only the range values of $g$ that are a part of the domain of $f$ are used. Thus, $f(g(x))$ isn't necessarily the same thing as $g(f(x))$, because often these functions might have different domains and ranges. We can also combine these two to create one function by substituting the input function into the where the $x$ is for the outer function. For instance, suppose you have the function $f(g(x))$ where $f(x) = 2x + 3$ and $g(x) = 3x + 4$. Now, input $g(x)$ into where $x$ is in $f(x)$. Thus, we have $f(g(x)) = 2(3x + 4) + 3$, which becomes $f(g(x)) = 6x + 11$. Let's call this composition function $h(x)$. To confirm if our model is correct, let's use the $x$-value of 7. $g(7)$ is 25, and $f(25)$ is 53. Now, $h(7)$ also gives us 53. Thus, $f(g(x)) = 6x + 11$. Interestingly, for a composition $f(g(x))$ or $g(f(x))$, if $f(x) = x$ (the parent linear function), then the composition will just be equal to $g(x)$. To prove this, in the case of $g(f(x))$, if $f(x) = x$, then we can substitute $x$ in the place of $f(x)$, so $g(f(x)) = g(x)$. In the case of $f(g(x))$, remember that $x$ is just the input value. So, when $f(x) = x$, that means that whatever you input into the function will be the output. Thus, if our input is $g(x)$, then our output will also be $g(x)$, so $f(g(x)) = g(f(x)) = g(x)$. One last idea to know is how to make one function into a composition of two or more functions. Let's say you have a function $h(x) = ax + b$. To make this a composition, we can make two new functions, one for each part of $h(x)$. First, we make a function $f(x) = ax$, and another function $g(x) = x + b$. Now, the composition

31

$g(f(x))$ will be equal to $ax + b$. In general, when we want to make a composition, we can just make two or more new functions that each account for a transformation in the function.

Now we're onto inverse functions. These are where you take the initial function and swap the x and y values in order to form a new function. Graphically, we're reflecting the function across the line $y = x$. In some cases, we may have to restrict the domain of the initial function in order to make the inverse of it also a function. For instance, for $f(x) = x^2$, reflecting it across the line $y = x$ creates a sideways parabola, which fails the vertical line test and is thus not a function. So, we usually restrict the domain of $x^2$ to $[0, \infty)$ in order to allow the inverse to be a function. To see if our initial function can be made into an inverse function, use the horizontal line test, as this is the equivalent of using the vertical line test on the inverse function. In some cases, we may have to restrict the domain of the initial function (range of the inverse) based on the real world context of the problem, so keep that in mind.

Now let's discuss how to create an inverse function. Suppose you had a function $f(x)$ with point $(a, b)$. The inverse function, $f^{-1}(x)$ would thus have the point $(b, a)$, and thus we swap the inputs and outputs when creating the inverse function. To find the inverse function, first get the equation of the function and use y instead of $f(x)$. Then, swap the $x$ and the $y$. After that, solve for $y$. Here's what that would look like for $f(x) = 5x + 17$

$$f(x) = 5x + 17$$
$$y = 5x + 17$$
$$x = 5y + 17$$
$$x - 17 = 5y$$
$$\frac{x - 17}{5} = f^{-1}(x)$$

Thus, our inverse function is $f^{-1}(x) = \frac{x-17}{5}$. Here's another one: $f(x) = \frac{-2}{3x+5}$. This is what the solution looks like:

$$f(x) = \frac{-2}{3x + 5}$$
$$y = \frac{-2}{3x + 5}$$
$$x = \frac{-2}{3y + 5}$$
$$3y + 5 = \frac{-2}{x}$$
$$3y = \frac{-2 - 5x}{x}$$
$$f^{-1}(x) = \frac{-2 - 5x}{3x}$$

Now, how do we know we did this correctly? We could of course plug in a point, but there is another method. The composition of a function and its inverse always is equal to x. This of course makes sense, as if x becomes y through the initial function, and y becomes x through the inverse, then x should stay as x through the composition. So, let's make the composition for our function here.

$$f(f^{-1}(x)) = \frac{-2}{3\left(\frac{-2 - 5x}{3x}\right) + 5}$$

$$f(f^{-1}(x)) = \frac{-2}{\left(\frac{-2-5x}{x}\right)+5}$$

$$f(f^{-1}(x)) = \frac{-2}{\left(\frac{-2}{x}\right)}$$

$$f(f^{-1}(x)) = x$$

Thus, to confirm if an inverse is correct, just create the composition and see if the result is x. Note that this works irrespective of if you do $f(f^{-1}(x))$ or $f^{-1}(f(x))$, but it's important that both $f(f^{-1}(x))$ and $f^{-1}(f(x))$ are x, not just one or the other.

## Practice Problems

*All 3 of the following questions are to be done without the use of a calculator*

1. Mark owns a store that sells fans. The function that gives the cost, in dollars, of buying x fans is known to be $f(x) = 4x + 16$, given that x is at least 1. However, on Mondays, Mark gives a discount given by the function $d(x) = 0.75x - 2$, where d is the final cost after the discount and x is the cost of the fans prior to the discount. Which of the following the gives the function $h(x)$, which gives the total cost of the fans after the Monday discount in terms of how many fans are bought?

   a. $h(x) = 3x + 14$

   b. $h(x) = 5.3x + 19.3$

   c. $h(x) = 3x + 10$

   d. $h(x) = 4x + 14$

2. James and Bill each wrote a function $f(x)$ and $g(x)$ respectively, where $f(x) = 4x - 6$ and $g(x) = -x + 5$. A third friend, Michael, decided to produce the function $h(x)$, made from the composition $f(g(x))$. After that, Michael graphed this composition function and reflected it across the parent function of the linear function, also known as $y = x$. Which of the following gives the proper equation for $h^{-1}(x)$, the function produced after reflecting $h(x)$ across the line y=x?

   a. $h^{-1}(x) = -x - 1$

   b. $h^{-1}(x) = \frac{-4x+20}{5}$

   c. $h^{-1}(x) = -4x + 14$

   d. $h^{-1}(x) = \frac{-x+14}{4}$

3. You made a regression line through a dataset earlier and plotted the residuals on a residual plot, shown in figure 12. Which of the following gives the correct

interpretation of the appropriateness of the initial linear model, based on the residual plot?

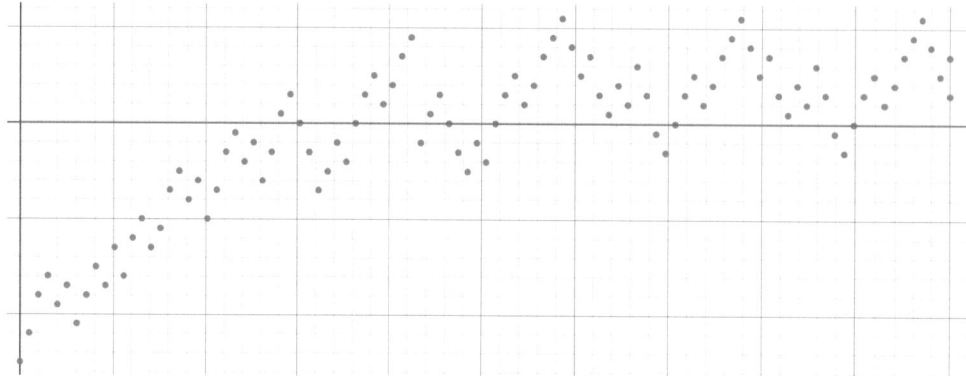

Figure 12 (1). This residual plot was made on Desmos.com.

a. The linear pattern is appropriate for the data, as there is a clear pattern in the residual plot

b. The linear pattern is appropriate for the data, as there is no clear pattern in the residual plot

c. The linear pattern is not appropriate for the data, as there is no clear pattern in the residual plot

d. The linear pattern is not appropriate for the data, as there is a clear pattern in the residual plot

## Solutions

1. This problem is essentially asking us to create a composition of functions, where our outside function is the discount function, and our inside function is the cost of fans function. Applying the discount function to the cost of fans function will give us 3x+10, so answer choice C is correct. If this is confusing, read back on the previous problems explained in this unit to understand how to create the composition.

2. In this problem, we are asked both to find the composition of the two functions and the inverse of that composition. First, for the inverse, we will get $h(x) = -4x + 14$. After that, we must take the inverse of this, which gets us $h^{-1}(x) = \frac{-x+14}{4}$. Thus, the correct answer choice is option D.

3. In this question, we need to analyze the residual plot to determine if there is a pattern, and then make the according conclusion. First off, it is evident that there is an increasing pattern in the residual plot. Thus, we can eliminate answer choices b and c. From there, we must remember the earlier idea that there should be no pattern in the residual plot if our model is accurate, as any variation in the residuals should be random and purely due to chance. Thus, the fact that there is a clear pattern in the residual plot means that the linear model is not the most appropriate for the data set, so D is the correct option.

# Module 6: Changes in Sequences and Functions

This next module focuses on sequences. A sequence is a set of successive numbers that follow a pattern and can be made into a function. However, sequences have whole number terms, such as the 1st term or the 2nd term, but not non-integer terms, such as the 1.5th term, and thus sequences aren't drawn with a line going through them, but instead just as points. The first sequence type that we'll look at is arithmetic sequences. In these sequences, the terms have a common difference, and thus it's basically like a linear function. The actual formula to find out a term from the arithmetic sequence is $a_n = a_0 + dn$, where $a_0$ is the initial value, so think of this like a y intercept, d is the common difference, and n is the term you are looking for, so if you want the 7th term, then n is 7. The linear equivalent of this is $y = b + mx$, where our y intercept of b is the same as $a_0$, our slope of m is the same as our common difference d, and our x value now is the nth term. There is another formula as well, and that is $a_n = a_k + d(n - k)$, and in this case $a_k$ is the $k$th term. If you really think about it, it's the same formula as the previous one, and just the previous one has $k = 0$. If you are given the 7th term, know the common difference to be 4, and want to find the 12th term, you would substitute $n$ is 12, $k$ is 7, $d$ is 4, and then solve. Let's do a sample problem. Suppose we have the arithmetic sequence 11, 15, 19, etc. What is the 13th term in the sequence? We know that 11 here is our first term, and thus it is $a_1$. Also, we can tell that our common difference is 4, as $19 - 15$ is 4 and $15 - 11$ is 4, and from the question we know that we are looking for the 13th term. Let's plug these values into our formula.

$$a_n = a_k + d(n - k)$$
$$a_{13} = 11 + 4(13 - 1)$$
$$a_{13} = 11 + 48$$
$$a_{13} = 59$$

Thus, the 13th term is 59. Relating this back to the idea of a linear function, given the line $y = 4x + 7$, when x is 13, y is 59. The reason that our y intercept is 7 and not 11 is because 11 is the first term, and so that means when x is 1, y is 11. However, y intercepts happen when x is 0, and thus we must subtract 4 from 11 to get our y intercept, thus 7.

Also, to find the sum of a given number of terms for an arithmetic sequence, use the following formula: $S_n = \frac{(a_k + a_n)(n - k + 1)}{2}$, where $a_k$ is the smallest term, $a_n$ is the largest term, and $S_n$ is the sum. Thus, you take the average value of a term $(\frac{a_k + a_n}{2})$ and multiply it by the number of terms $(n - k + 1)$. Thus, for the sequence 2, 4, 6, 8, 10, the sum is 30.

The other type of sequences is geometric sequences. In this case, rather than a common difference between successive terms, we have a common ratio. In other words, if you divide the 2nd term by the 1st term, it should be equal to the 3rd term divided by the 2nd term. The formula in this case is $g_n = g_0 r^n$, or alternatively $g_n = g_k r^{n-k}$. Just as how arithmetic sequences were related to linear functions, geometric sequences are related to exponential functions. In this case, $g_n = g_0 r^n$ converts to $y = ab^x$, where $a$ matches $g_0$ (the initial value), $b$ matches $r$ (the common ratio), and $x$ matches $n$ (the input value). Let's do an example. Given the geometric sequence 3, 6, 12, etc., what is the 7th term? We know that we are looking for the 7th term, the common ratio is 2 (12 divided by 6 is 2, 6 divided by 3 is 2), and we know 3 is $g_1$. Let's use the formula now.

$$g_n = g_k r^{(n-k)}$$
$$g_7 = (3)2^{(7-1)}$$

$$g_7 = (3)64$$
$$g_7 = 192$$

Thus, the 7th term of the sequence is 192. To relate this back to exponential functions, given the equation $y = 1.5(2)^x$, for the $x$ value of 7, $y$ is 192. To find the sum of a geometric series, use the following formula: $S_n = \frac{a_1(r^n-1)}{r-1}$, where $a_1$ is the first term, $r$ is the common ratio, and n is the final term. Thus, for the sequence 2, 4, 8, 16, 32, the sum would be 62. Interestingly, in some cases, it is possible to find the sum of the infinite series. If the $r$ value is under 1, then using the formula $S = \frac{a_1}{1-r}$, you can find the sum. However, if the $r$ value is above 1, each term would be bigger than the last, and thus the sum would reach infinity. Using the previous formula, for the sequence $1 + \frac{1}{2} + \frac{1}{4} + \frac{1}{8} + \frac{1}{16} + \ldots$, the sum is 2.

Finally, as for the distinction between a sequence and a series, a sequence, as said earlier, is a string of successive numbers, such as 1, 2, 3, 4. A series, on the other hand, is a sum of these successive numbers, so it would be $1 + 2 + 3 + 4$.

## Practice Problems

*A graphing calculator is permitted for the following questions*

1. Given an arithmetic sequence with an initial value of 4 and a common difference of 5, which of the following gives the linear function $f(n)$ for the nth term, along with the 12th term in the sequence?

    a. $f(n) = 5n - 4$; 56

    b. $f(n) = 5n + 4$; 64

    c. $f(n) = 4n - 5$; 43

    d. $f(n) = 4n + 5$; 53

2. Consider an arithmetic series where $a_1 = 3$ and $d = 7$. Which of the following represents $S_n$, the sum of the first n terms of the series?

    a. $S_n = 7n + 3$

    b. $S_n = 7n - 3$

    c. $S_n = \frac{n(7n-1)}{2}$

    d. $S_n = \frac{7n(n-1)}{2}$

3. Given the exponential function $g(n) = 5(3)^x$, which of the following gives the correct initial value and common ratio?

    a. $a_1 = 3, r = 5$

b.  $a_1 = 5, r = 3$

c.  $a_0 = 3, r = 5$

d.  $a_0 = 5, r = 3$

## Solutions

1.  As explained in the module, when converting an arithmetic series to a linear equation, the initial value becomes the y intercept while the common difference becomes the slope, and thus the correct linear equation is $f(n) = 5n + 4$. Plugging in 12 for $n$ gets us 64, and thus b is the correct answer choice.

2.  Using the formula, it is known that to find the sum of an arithmetic series, the formula $S_n = \frac{n(a_1 + a_n)}{2}$. However, we do not know what $a_n$ is, so we must solve for that. Using an earlier formula $a_n = a_1 + d(n-1)$, we can substitute that into the equation, giving us $S_n = \frac{n(a_1 + a_1 + d(n-1))}{2}$. From there, we can just substitute the values from the question, that being $a_1$ is 3 and $d$ is 7, eventually leading us to the equation $S_n = \frac{n(7n-1)}{2}$, and thus the correct answer choice is option c.

3.  As explained in the module, the general form of an exponential function is $g(n) = ab^x$, where a is the initial value, b is the common ratio, and $x$ is the input value. Using this information, we can see that 5 corresponds to $a_0$ and 3 corresponds to b, and thus 5 is $a_0$ and 3 is $b$, so the correct answer is option d.

# Module 7: Exponential Functions

Following the discussion of geometric sequences, this module covers exponential functions. The standard form is $f(x) = ab^x$, where $a \neq 0$ and $b > 0$ but $b \neq 1$. The reason for these conditions is that if $a$ was 0, the whole function would be 0, and if $b$ was 1, the whole function would just be $a$, and finally $b > 0$ because if $b$ was a negative number, $x$-values such as ½ or 2.5 would yield non-real $y$-values. If $a$ is positive and $b > 1$, then the function shows exponential growth, while if $a > 0$ and $0 < b < 1$, the function shows exponential decay.

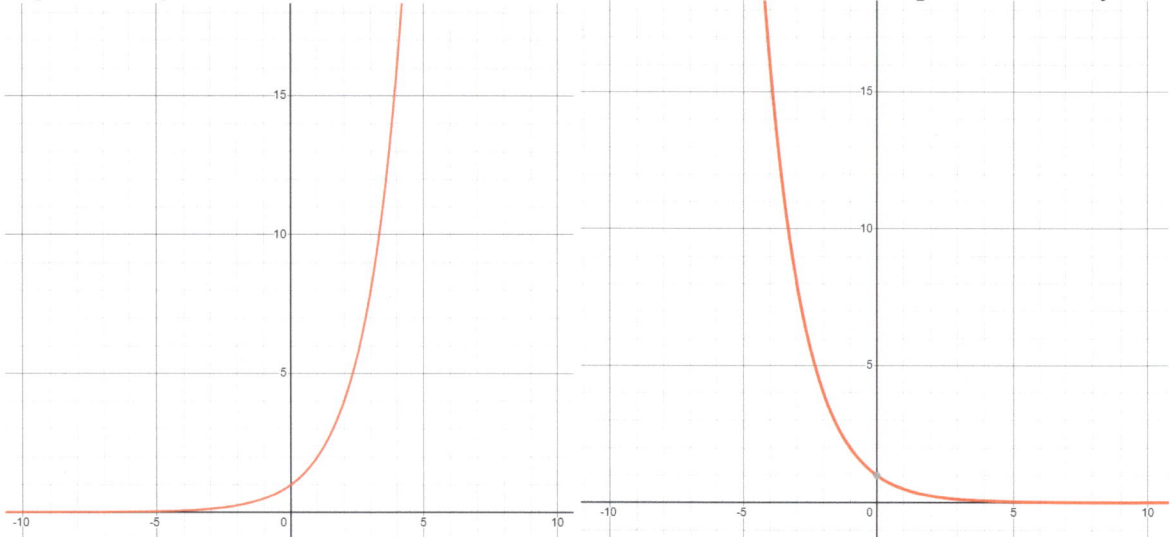

Figure 13 (1). The image above is from Desmos.com. The image on the left is from the graph $y = 2^x$ and demonstrates exponential growth, while the one on the right is $y = 0.5^x$ and demonstrates exponential decay.

From observing the graphs of these functions, it's clear that the function and its rate of change is either always increasing or decreasing, because $y$-values remain proportional over equal $x$ intervals. Tying this back to module 1, this means that exponential functions are always concave up or concave down. If $a$ is positive, then the function is concave up, but if $a$ is negative, then the function is concave down. Furthermore, unlike quadratics which have a maximum or minimum, or cubics which have clear inflection points, exponential functions do not have a maximum or minimum, but if you make a closed interval, then they could have absolute minima and maxima. Thus, for an exponential function in the form $y = ab^x$, as $x$ approaches positive or negative infinity, the $y$ values approach either negative infinity, 0, or infinity depending on the function. For instance, for the function $f(x) = 3(4)^x$, as $x$ approaches positive infinity, $y$ approaches positive infinity, but as $x$ approaches negative infinity, $y$ approaches 0. In limit notation, this would be $\lim\limits_{x \to \infty} 3(4)^x = \infty$ and $\lim\limits_{x \to -\infty} 3(4)^x = 0$. For the function $f(x) = -2(0.5)^x$, as $x$ approaches negative infinity, $y$ approaches negative infinity, but as $x$ approaches positive infinity, $y$ approaches 0. Or, in limit notation, $\lim\limits_{x \to \infty} -2(0.5)^x = 0$ and $\lim\limits_{x \to -\infty} -2(0.5)^x = -\infty$

Also, if you have an exponential function, it remains exponential even after adding constants to it. Thus, if $f(x) = 2^x$ (and thus is exponential), then $g(x) = f(x) + 3$, will also be exponential. However, because $g(x)$ isn't in standard form, then as $x$ approaches negative infinity, $y$ will approach 3, not 0, though it will still approach positive infinity as $x$ approaches positive infinity.

Continuing our focus on transformations, we must now discuss how the different properties of exponents affect the graph. First off, exponential functions in standard form are as follows: $y = a(b^{cx+h}) + k$, where $h$ is the horizontal shift, $k$ is the vertical shift, $a$ is responsible for vertical dilations, and $c$ is responsible for horizontal dilations. The product property of exponents states that $p^a p^b = p^{a+b}$, and so if we compare this to the $b^{x+h}$ from the standard form, we realize that we can expand out $b^{x+h}$ to become $b^x b^h$, and because $b^h$ is a constant, this means that a horizontal shift also constitutes as a vertical dilation, if we consider $b^h$ to be a part of the $a$ value of the function. Similarly, the power property of exponents states that $(p^a)^b = p^{ab}$, and this can then be converted into $(p^b)^a$. If we relate this to the $b^{cx}$ portion of the graph equation, this means that a horizontal dilation by $c$ is also a change in base, as the function could be considered $(b^c)^x$, where $b^c$ is the base of the function rather than just $b$.

For some other general exponential properties, $p^{-a} = \dfrac{1}{p^a}$, and to relate this to the function, if we have a negative exponent, then we form a fraction that has the part of the number with a negative exponent in the denominator. Thus, $b^{-x+2}$ becomes $\dfrac{b^2}{b^x}$. Also, $p^{\frac{1}{a}} = \sqrt[a]{p}$, and when using this property on the function, if given $b^{\frac{1}{x}+h}$, you can convert this to $\sqrt[x]{b^{hx+1}}$.

Another concept relating to exponential functions is that of the number $e$. $e$ is a mathematical constant approximately equal to 2.718, and is similar to $\pi$ in that it is an irrational number. One way to derive the value of $e$ is the following: $\lim\limits_{n \to \infty} \left(1 + \dfrac{1}{n}\right)^n = e$. The importance of $e$ is that it is often considered the natural log or the natural base for exponential functions, and many functions use $e$ as a base. If you are evaluating something that is continuously growing, you use $e$ as the base.

Finally, it is important to discuss uses for exponential functions. In certain cases, you can infer what the function means based on how it is represented. For instance, if $f(x) = 100(1.1^w)$, where $w$ represents how many weeks have gone by and $f$ gives the amount of money earned in a bank account, then this means that the account gains 10% interest every week. However, if the function is represented $f(x) = 100(1.1^{52})^{\frac{w}{52}}$, this means that every 52 weeks, or in other words, every year, the value of the account multiplies by $1.1^{52}$. Mathematically, this is equivalent to the previous function, but now it has a different meaning.

## Practice Problems

*A graphing calculator is permitted for the following questions*

1. A certain type of bacteria grows exponentially at a rate of 8% per hour. If the initial population size is 100, which of the following functions best expresses the population of the bacteria, $P(h)$, after $h$ hours?

    a. $P(h) = 100(1.08)^h$

    b. $P(h) = 100(0.08)^h$

c. $P(h) = 100(1.08)^{0.08h}$

d. $P(h) = 100(0.92)^{h}$

2. A population of rabbits is estimated to grow at an exponential rate of approximately 10% every 3 years. After 15 years, which of the following will be true, given that the population size was initially 50?

   a. There will be 55 rabbits.

   b. There will be 209 rabbits.

   c. There will be 80 rabbits.

   d. There will be 67 rabbits.

3. Given $f(x) = 2^x$ and $g(x) = 3^x$, which of the following gives $g(f(2))$?

   a. 512

   b. 64

   c. 243

   d. 81

## Solutions

1. In this problem, we are told that the population is growing at a rate of 8% per hour. 8%=0.08, and because it is growing, that means the base for the exponential function is 1.08, as whenever there is growth you must add the rate to 1. From there, we know that the growth happens per hour, and thus the h in the exponent should be alone. Thus, a is the correct answer.

2. In this problem, we must directly find the population size. We must use the following expression to solve: $f(15) = 50(1.1^{\frac{15}{3}})$, which comes out to approximately 80. Thus, c is the correct answer.

3. To solve this composition of functions, we simply substitute 2 into $f(x)$, and then the resulting $y$-value into $g(x)$. $f(2) = 4$, and $g(4) = 81$, and thus answer choice d is the correct option.

# Module 8: Logarithmic Functions

The previous module was centered on exponential functions, wherein as the $x$-values change additively, meaning one by one, the $y$-values change multiplicatively. In this module, were going to discuss the opposite: logarithms, wherein as the $x$-values change multiplicatively, the $y$-values change additively. Logarithms are in the form $\log_b c$, where $b$, the base, is larger than 0 but not 1, and $c$ is a constant. A logarithm solves for an exponent. In other words, $\log_b c$ means the power that $b$ must be raised to in order to equal $c$. Thus, if $\log_b c = a$, then $b^a = c$. In fact, logarithms are the inverse functions of exponentials, meaning that a composition of the two would equal $x$ and reflecting one across the line $y = x$ produces the other function, also meaning that if the point $(p, q)$ is on the exponential, the point $(q, p)$ will be on the logarithm. Just like exponentials, logarithms do not have extrema unless it is on a closed interval and are always concave up or down with no inflection points.

A horizontal shift to a logarithmic function may cause the input values to no longer be proportional, but the function will remain logarithmic. Thus, if a function created by a horizontal shift is logarithmic, then that means the initial function was also logarithmic.

If the logarithm was not horizontally shifted, then it has a vertical asymptote at $x = 0$. This makes sense, as in exponential functions, there's a horizontal asymptote at $y = 0$, and the logarithm function is a reflection of the exponential function across $y = x$. Furthermore, it's impossible for the base to multiply out to reach 0, as it will always have some small value, resulting in the vertical asymptote seen at $x = 0$. As $x$ approaches positive infinity, $y$ approaches positive or negative infinity, albeit very slowly. In limit notation, this is $\lim_{x \to \infty} \log_b x = -\infty$ or $\lim_{x \to \infty} \log_b x = \infty$, respectively.

Just like exponents, there are also certain properties of logarithms that can be applied to the function. The first is the product property, which states that $\log_a bc = \log_a b + \log_a c$, meaning that a horizontal dilation in the form $\log_a bx$ becomes $\log_a b + \log_a x$, and thus the horizontal dilation becomes a vertical shift, as if we substitute $k = \log_a b$, we have $\log_a x + k$. The power property states that $\log_a x^b = b \log_a x$, meaning that raising the power of the input causes a vertical dilation. The change of base property states that $\log_a b = \frac{\log_c a}{\log_c b}$, where $c > 0$ but not 1. Using this idea, with the realization that $\log_a b$ is a constant, then changing the base constitutes as a vertical dilation. Also, using the definition of a logarithm, in that it is the exponent the base needs to equal the argument, if you write $2^{\log_2 10}$, it will be equal to 10. In general, whenever you see a number in this format, wherein the base of the exponential portion of the number is equal to the base of the log, the number will be equal to the argument of the logarithm. Or, in the words of numerous students, "cancel out" these bases to find the value of the expression.

There are two special logarithms. Logarithms with a base of 10 are called common logarithms. Because it is the common log, its normally written without the base 10 being there, so if you see an equation that simply says log without a base number, it means log base 10. The other one is ln, which is log base $e$. As said earlier, this is the natural log, and thus if you see $\ln x$, it means log base $e$ of $x$. Also, $e^{\ln x}$ is equal to $x$, using the earlier rule of when the base of the logarithm and the exponential expression are the same.

Finally, we must discuss semi-log plots. These are graphs where one of the axes is logarithmically scaled, meaning that rather than going additively, such as 1, 2, 3, the axis would go in exponential order, such as $10^1$, $10^2$, and $10^3$. This is useful because data that would normally appear as exponential now appears linear. Thus, you won't have to employ techniques such as adding constants to the $y$-values or performing dilations in order to ensure that an exponential model is appropriate, as verifying if the semi-log plot is linear ensures that the function is an exponential. Specifically, if you have an exponential model $y = ab^x$, the graph of the line you would use in the semi-log plot would be $y = (\log_c b)x + \log_c a$, where $c > 0$ and $c \neq 1$, and thus the slope is $\log_c b$ and the y intercept is $\log_c a$.

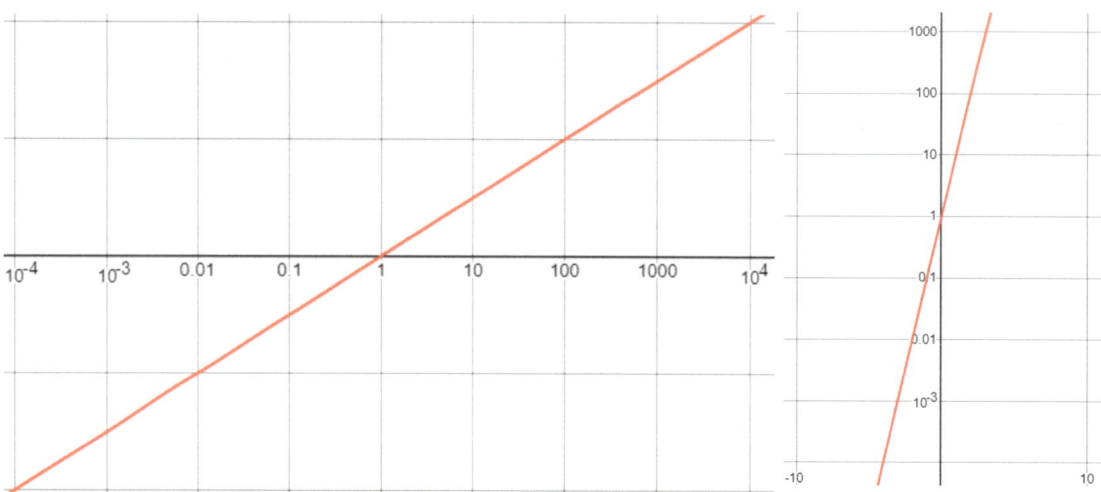

Figures 14 (1) and 15(1). These graphs are both from Desmos.com. The graph on the left is of the function $y = \log x$, which is the common log, while the one on the right is of $y = 10^x$. Notice how for figure 13, $x$-axis values do not increase in a linear fashion, but rather change multiplicatively, while the $y$-values, not pictured, change additively. On the other hand, for figure 14, the $x$-values change additively while the $y$-values change multiplicatively. In both cases, by changing one of the axes, the once-curved function now is linear, thus demonstrating how semi-log plots can help confirm if a function is truly exponential or logarithmic.

## Practice Problems

*All 3 of the following questions are to be done without the use of a graphing calculator*

1. Which of the following gives the correct logarithmic equation for the exponential equation $3^4 = 81$?

    a. $\log_4 3 = 81$

    b. $\log_4 81 = 3$

    c. $\log_3 4 = 81$

    d. $\log_3 81 = 4$

2. Given that $\log_a 4 = 2$ and $\log_a 5 = 2.609$, find the value of $\log_a 20$.

    a. 5.218

b. 4.609

c. 0.609

d. 6.807

3. Consider the equation $y = b^x$. Which of the following describes the proper type of semi-log plot that should be used to graph its <u>inverse</u> and why?

a. A semi-log plot with the $x$-axis on a logarithmic scale and the $y$-axis on a linear scale would be the most appropriate to graph the inverse because the inverse is an exponential equation, wherein $y$-values increase multiplicatively while $x$-values increase linearly, and thus the $x$ axis needs to be on a logarithmic scale to combat this difference.

b. A semi-log plot with the $x$-axis on a linear scale and the $y$-axis on a logarithmic scale would be the most appropriate to graph the inverse because the inverse is an exponential equation, wherein $y$-values increase multiplicatively while $x$-values increase linearly, and thus the $y$ axis needs to be a logarithmic scale to combat this difference.

c. A semi-log plot with the $x$-axis on a logarithmic scale and the $y$-axis on a linear scale would be the most appropriate to graph the inverse because the inverse is a logarithmic equation, wherein $x$-values increase multiplicatively while $y$-values increase linearly, and thus the $x$ axis needs to be on a logarithmic scale to combat this difference.

d. A semi-log plot with the $x$-axis on a linear scale and the $y$-axis on a logarithmic scale would be the most appropriate to graph the inverse because the inverse is a logarithmic equation, wherein $x$-values increase multiplicatively while $y$-values increase linearly, and thus the y axis needs to be on a logarithmic scale to combat this difference.

## Solutions

1. In this question, we are asked to convert the exponential form of this equation to the logarithmic form. Remember that a logarithmic equation solves for the exponent, and thus the right side of the equal sign should have a 4, as that is the exponent shown in the logarithm. Furthermore, the base of the logarithm should be the same of the exponential, and thus 3. Finally, the argument of the logarithm should be the same as the "answer" of the exponential, and thus 81. The answer choice that follows all 3 of these requirements is choice d, and thus option d is the correct answer.

2. In this question, we are asked to use properties of logarithms to find the solution. In this case, we must use the properties $\log_a bc = \log_a b + \log_a c$, and in this case, our b is 4 and c is 5. Thus, to find $\log_a 20$, we must add $\log_a 4$ to $\log_a 5$. This is equal to adding 2 and 2.609, and thus our answer is 4.609, which is choice b.

3. In this question, we are asked to determine the proper semi-log plot for the inverse of an exponential. The inverse of an exponential equation is a logarithmic equation, and thus we can eliminate choices a and b. From there, in a logarithmic equation, it is the $x$-values that increase multiplicatively and the $y$-values that increase linearly. In order to convert this into a linear equation, which is the intent of a semi-log plot, we must alter the $x$ axis to also be linear, and thus c is the correct choice.

# Unit 3: Trigonometric and Polar Functions

- Module 9: Trigonometric Basics: Sine, Cosine, and Tangent

- Module 10: Sinusoidal Functions, Graphing, and Modeling

- Module 11: Tangent Functions, Inverse and Reciprocal Trigonometric Functions

- Module 12: Simplifying and Solving Trigonometric Equations

- Module 13: Polar Functions

# Module 9: Trigonometric Basics: Sine, Cosine, and Tangent

To start off this trigonometric unit, we must talk about a characteristic key to their graphs: periodicity. For a function to be periodic means that for successive equal length intervals, the function repeats and has the same pattern. The period itself is defined as the smallest positive value $k$ such that $f(x + k) = f(x)$ for every $x$-value. In other words, $k$ is the length of the period, and thus if you move $k$ units to the right of a given point, the point will have the same $y$-value. Every period is identical, so whatever happens in one period, be it concaving up or down, curving, etc., will happen in every period.

To introduce our trigonometric functions, we must also describe angles in the coordinate plane and the unit circle. An angle in standard position is one in which one of the rays is on the positive x axis and the vertex is at the origin. The other ray is the terminal ray, and the angle between the rays is measured positively in the counterclockwise direction, and negatively in the clockwise direction. When discussing angles, we usually measure them in either degrees or radians. Throughout this course, we will be using radians, although it is good to know degree measures in case it helps you to understand better. When an angle shares a terminal ray with another angle, those angles are $2\pi n$ from one another, where $n$ is an integer. This means that they are an integer number of revolutions away from each other. To convert from degrees to radians, multiply the degree measure by $\frac{\pi}{180}$. To find the radian measure of the angle without already knowing the angle, its the length of the arc of the circle created by the angle divided by the radius, thus explaining why we get measures such as $\pi$ radians. Another way of thinking about it is what is the arclength in terms of radii. In the case of the unit circle, the radius is 1, and so the arc length is the same thing as the angle measure in radians.

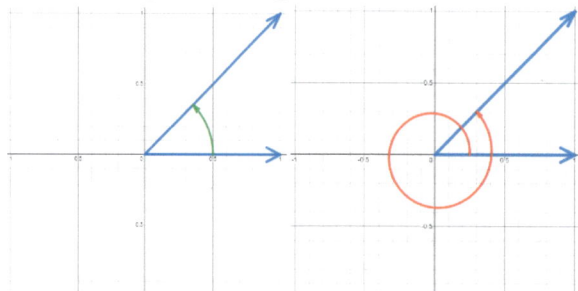

Figures 16 (1) and 17 (1). These graphs were made on Desmos.com. Both graphs display an angle in standard position, though note that angles do not have to be in the first quadrant like these two are. Both angles are measured positively, because they are measured in the counterclockwise direction, but the angle on the right includes a revolution of $2\pi$ along with the measure of the angle.

Sine, as you may have learned in geometry, is the ratio of the side opposite of the angle to the hypotenuse. When looking at a standard position angle in the unit circle, the radius of the circle forms part of the terminal ray, and it connects with the circumference at some point B, with coordinates $(x, y)$. We can create a triangle here with the radius as the hypotenuse, the x axis as one of the legs, and a third side parallel to the y axis to connect the other two sides together. If we evaluate sine of this standard position angle, it would be the length of the opposite side divided by the hypotenuse, which in this case is the $y$-value of the point divided by 1. Thus, sine of a standard position angle in the unit circle is the $y$ coordinate of the point B.

Following similar logic, cosine gives the $x$ coordinate of the point B. The reason is because cosine is the ratio of the adjacent side to the hypotenuse, and in this case, the adjacent side gives the $x$-value of the point B, and the hypotenuse is 1, so thus cosine of the standard position angle gives the $x$ coordinate of the point.

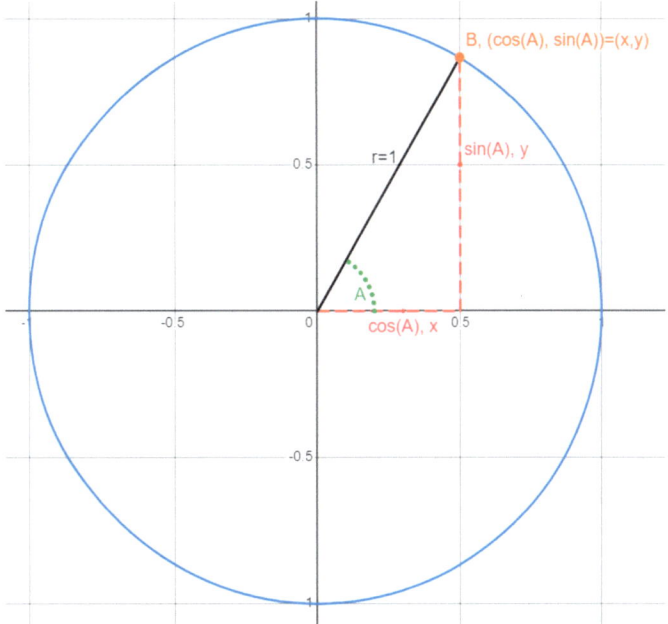

Figure 18 (1). This graph was made on Desmos.com. Within the unit circle, an angle is shown in standard position with measure A. The orange point on the circle has coordinates (cos A, sin A). Because the radius of the circle is 1, the side lengths of the triangle are cos(A), sin(A), and 1, and thus because of this unit circle, we can now think of angles in terms of the coordinate plane, allowing us to graph trigonometric functions.

Using these two ideas, we can rewrite a point on the unit circle as $(\cos\theta, \sin\theta)$. In the case of points not on the unit circle that lie on a circumference of another circle also centered on the origin, they can be referred to as $(r\cos\theta, r\sin\theta)$, where $r$ is the radius of the circle and $\theta$ is the measure of the angle in standard position.

Finally tangent gives the slope of the terminal ray. Because tangent is dividing opposite by adjacent, and opposite is the $y$-value while adjacent is the $x$-value, tangent is essentially dividing $y$ by $x$, which is known to be the slope, and by extension the ratio of the sine to cosine for the given angle.

As for specific values of these angles, the exact sine and cosine values can be found for multiples of $\frac{\pi}{6}$ and $\frac{\pi}{4}$. This is because of the properties of isosceles right triangles and equilateral triangles. The following tables give the sine, cosine, and tangent measures for these angles.

| Angle | 0 | $\frac{\pi}{6}$ | $\frac{\pi}{4}$ | $\frac{\pi}{3}$ | $\frac{\pi}{2}$ | $\frac{2\pi}{3}$ | $\frac{3\pi}{4}$ | $\frac{5\pi}{6}$ | $\pi$ |
|---|---|---|---|---|---|---|---|---|---|
| Sine | 0 | $\frac{1}{2}$ | $\frac{\sqrt{2}}{2}$ | $\frac{\sqrt{3}}{2}$ | 1 | $\frac{\sqrt{3}}{2}$ | $\frac{\sqrt{2}}{2}$ | $\frac{1}{2}$ | 0 |
| Cosine | 1 | $\frac{\sqrt{3}}{2}$ | $\frac{\sqrt{2}}{2}$ | $\frac{1}{2}$ | 0 | $-\frac{1}{2}$ | $-\frac{\sqrt{2}}{2}$ | $-\frac{\sqrt{3}}{2}$ | $-1$ |

| Tangent | 0 | $\dfrac{\sqrt{3}}{3}$ | 1 | $\sqrt{3}$ | Undefined | $-\sqrt{3}$ | -1 | $-\dfrac{\sqrt{3}}{3}$ | 0 |
|---|---|---|---|---|---|---|---|---|---|

| Angle | $\dfrac{7\pi}{6}$ | $\dfrac{5\pi}{4}$ | $\dfrac{4\pi}{3}$ | $\dfrac{3\pi}{2}$ | $\dfrac{5\pi}{3}$ | $\dfrac{7\pi}{4}$ | $\dfrac{11\pi}{6}$ | $2\pi$ |
|---|---|---|---|---|---|---|---|---|
| Sine | $-\dfrac{1}{2}$ | $-\dfrac{\sqrt{2}}{2}$ | $-\dfrac{\sqrt{3}}{2}$ | -1 | $-\dfrac{\sqrt{3}}{2}$ | $-\dfrac{\sqrt{2}}{2}$ | $-\dfrac{1}{2}$ | 0 |
| Cosine | $-\dfrac{\sqrt{3}}{2}$ | $-\dfrac{\sqrt{2}}{2}$ | $-\dfrac{1}{2}$ | 0 | $\dfrac{1}{2}$ | $\dfrac{\sqrt{2}}{2}$ | $\dfrac{\sqrt{3}}{2}$ | 1 |
| Tangent | $\dfrac{\sqrt{3}}{3}$ | 1 | $\sqrt{3}$ | Undefined | $-\sqrt{3}$ | -1 | $-\dfrac{\sqrt{3}}{3}$ | 0 |

These angles are very commonly used when solving problems relating to the unit circle and trigonometry, so it is important to remember these values. At first, that may seem daunting as there are so many value.. However, upon looking at the tables, some clear patterns emerge. For instance, sine and cosine use the same values, just at different points. Thus, $\sin(\theta + \frac{\pi}{2}) = \cos(\theta)$. Also, the numbers themselves are in a pattern. If we focus on the values of sine, and we consider 0 to be $\frac{\sqrt{0}}{2}$, $\frac{1}{2}$ to be $\frac{\sqrt{1}}{2}$, and 1 to be $\frac{\sqrt{4}}{2}$, then the values of sine and cosine are halves the square roots of the numbers 0 through 4. The reason tangent is undefined at 2 angles ($\frac{\pi}{2}$ and $\frac{3\pi}{2}$) is because at those points, cosine is 0, and because tangent is formed by dividing sine by cosine, the tangent values at those two angles would be $\frac{1}{0}$ and $\frac{-1}{0}$, respectively. Of course, dividing by zero is undefined, and thus tangent at those two angles is undefined. To understand why these angles increase and decrease at this pattern, let's take another look at the unit circle in figure 19.

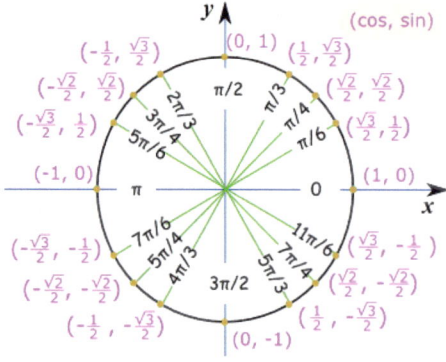

Figure 19 (2). This image is taken from Math.stackexchange.com. It shows the coordinate values, and thus the sine and cosine values, of different angles along the unit circle.

In the image above, as we go along the unit circle, increasing our angle measure, we move along the circle, which explains why we have the same values repeating over and over again, as in a sense, all the angles shown here are made from the same two special right triangles in different orientations, and thus it would be the same side lengths, with the only differences coming from the axis that each side lies on and the orientation of the triangle. Also, initially we start at the far right of the circle, and as we increase our angle, we start to move left and up, thus explaining while sine increases and cosine decreases. We then continue to move left, but start to go down, thus causing both sine and cosine to decrease. However, in the third quadrant, we start to back towards the right, while we continue moving downwards, thus cosine increases while sine decreases. Finally, in the fourth quadrant, we move right and upwards, and thus sine and cosine both increase. With this understanding of patterns within the unit circle, it should now be much easier to remember all the basic angles and values.

## *Practice Problems*

*All 3 of the following questions are to be done without the use of a graphing calculator*

1. Consider an angle $\theta$ in standard position such that its terminal side passes through the point $(5, 12)$. Which of the following trigonometric ratios is correct for this angle?

   a. $\sin \theta = \frac{5}{12}$ and $\cos \theta = \frac{7}{12}$

   b. $\sin \theta = \frac{7}{12}$ and $\cos \theta = \frac{5}{12}$

   c. $\sin \theta = \frac{5}{13}$ and $\cos \theta = \frac{13}{12}$

   d. $\sin \theta = \frac{5}{13}$ and $\cos \theta = \frac{12}{13}$

2. Which of the following trigonometric value pairs is correct for $\frac{7\pi}{6}$ and $\frac{3\pi}{4}$?

   a. $\sin\left(\frac{7\pi}{6}\right) = -\frac{1}{2}$ and $\cos\left(\frac{3\pi}{4}\right) = -\frac{\sqrt{2}}{2}$

   b. $\sin\left(\frac{7\pi}{6}\right) = \frac{1}{2}$ and $\cos\left(\frac{3\pi}{4}\right) = -\frac{\sqrt{2}}{2}$

   c. $\sin\left(\frac{7\pi}{6}\right) = -\frac{1}{2}$ and $\cos\left(\frac{3\pi}{4}\right) = \frac{\sqrt{2}}{2}$

   d. $\sin\left(\frac{7\pi}{6}\right) = \frac{1}{2}$ and $\cos\left(\frac{3\pi}{4}\right) = \frac{\sqrt{2}}{2}$

3. Consider the point $P$ on the unit circle corresponding to an angle $\theta$ in standard position. If $P$ lies in the second quadrant, which of the following trigonometric values must be <u>false</u>?

a. $\sin\theta = \frac{\sqrt{3}}{2}$

b. $\cos\theta = \frac{1}{2}$

c. $\cos\theta = -\frac{\sqrt{2}}{2}$

d. $\tan\theta = -1$

# Solutions

1. In this question, we are asked to find the trigonometric values for a given point. Remember that for any point at the end of a line segment for a standard position angle, the coordinates of the point are in the form $(r\cos\theta, r\sin\theta)$. Thus, given the point (5, 12), we can find out the sine and cosine values by finding r. To find r, simply remember that we got these ratios from a right triangle, and thus we can use the Pythagorean theorem to solve for r. Because this is a special 5-12-13 triangle, we also know that the hypotenuse, which is r, is 13. Thus, we must divide 5 and 12 by 13 to get sine and cosine. Thus, option d is the correct answer.

2. In this question, we are asked to find the trigonometric values for a given unit circle angle. Thus, to find the answer, we can reference the table from earlier in the chapter and find that the correct answer is a. Alternatively, we can realize that because $\frac{7\pi}{6}$ is larger than $\pi$, sine must be negative, because from the interval $\pi$ to $2\pi$, non-inclusive, the values of sine are negative. Similarly, because $\frac{3\pi}{4}$ is larger than $\frac{\pi}{2}$, we know that cosine is negative, as from the interval $\frac{\pi}{2}$ to $\frac{3\pi}{2}$, cosine is negative. The only answer choice that has both the sine and cosine values as negative is a, and thus answer choice a must be the correct answer.

3. We are told that the point $P$ lies in the second quadrant. In the second quadrant, sine values are positive, cosine values are negative, and tangent values are negative. Thus, in order for an answer to be false, it must violate one of those three conditions. Answer choice B involves a positive cosine value, and thus it is false statement. Therefore, choice B is the correct answer.

# Module 10: Sinusoidal Functions, Graphing, and Modeling

Continuing our previous discussion of sine and cosine with the understanding of them in relation to the $x$ and $y$ axes, we can now focus on them in a graphical context. To start, the function $f(\theta) = \sin\theta$ gives the $y$-value for the input $\theta$, where $\theta$ is an angle in standard position. Thus, for $\theta = 0$, $f(\theta)$ is 0, and for $\theta = \frac{\pi}{2}$, $f(\theta) = 1$. The domain of the function is all real numbers, meaning that $\theta$ can be any real value. The range, however, is $[-1, 1]$ meaning that the minimum value of $y$ is $-1$, and the maximum value is 1. Similarly, the function $f(\theta) = \cos\theta$ gives the $x$-value for the input $\theta$, and thus for $\theta = 0$, $f(\theta)$ is 1, and for $\theta = \frac{\pi}{2}$, $f(\theta)$ is 0. Note that here, $f(\theta)$ is giving the $x$-value of the coordinate that would be formed by the angle $\theta$ in standard position. However, when the function is graphed, these "$x$" values are the $y$-values for the function, as in the coordinate plane, the function is written as $y = \cos x$, not $\cos\theta$.

Both of these functions are known as sinusoidal functions, which are functions based on transforming $f(x) = \sin x$, or in other words, $f(\theta) = \sin\theta$. The reason $f(x) = \cos x$ is considered sinusoidal is because $\cos\theta = \sin(\theta + \frac{\pi}{2})$, and thus cosine is a horizontal shift of sine. Because the graph of $y = \sin\theta$ has rotational symmetry about the origin, it is an odd function, while $y = \cos\theta$ is an even function because it has reflective symmetry about the y-axis.

The general forms of sinusoidal functions are $f(\theta) = a\sin\big(b(\theta + c)\big) + d$ and $g(\theta) = a\cos\big(b(\theta + c)\big) + d$, where $a \neq 0$. Using this general form, we can describe functions based on their transformations, which often have different terms for each one. A horizontal shift in the form $g(\theta) = \sin(\theta + c)$ is known as a phase shift, and in this case, it would be a phase shift by $-c$ units. Phase shifts alter where periods of the function start and stop, and the period of a function, as described earlier, is the shortest distance $k$ for which $f(x + k) = f(x)$ for all values of $x$. The period for both $\sin\theta$ and $\cos\theta$ is $2\pi$. The frequency is the number of periods that occur over an $x$-interval of 1 and is the reciprocal of the period. Thus, for both $\sin\theta$ and $\cos\theta$, the frequency is $\frac{1}{2\pi}$, meaning that 1 period happens every $2\pi$. These numbers are altered by horizontal dilations, which come in the form $g(\theta) = \sin(b\theta)$, and causes the period to change by a factor of $\left|\frac{1}{b}\right|$. For instance, $\sin 2\theta$ has a period of $\pi$, and thus a frequency of $\frac{1}{\pi}$. The amplitude is half of the difference between the maximum and minimum output values. In the case of $y = \sin\theta$, the amplitude is 1. The amplitude is altered by vertical dilations, which come in the form $g(\theta) = a\sin\theta$, with $|a|$ being the amplitude. For instance, $y = 2\sin\theta$ has an amplitude of 2. Finally, the midline of the graph is the average of the minimum and maximum values of the function, and if you draw a line at where the midline is, it should divide the function in half. The midline of $y = \sin\theta$ is $y = 0$. This can be altered by vertical shifts. For instance, $y = \sin\theta + 2$ has a midline at $y = 2$, and in general a vertical shift in the form $g(\theta) = \sin(\theta) + d$ is a vertical translation of the midline by $d$ units. Note that every single one of these transformations discussed applies the exact same way to the cosine function, as after all, the cosine function can be considered as a shifted sine function.

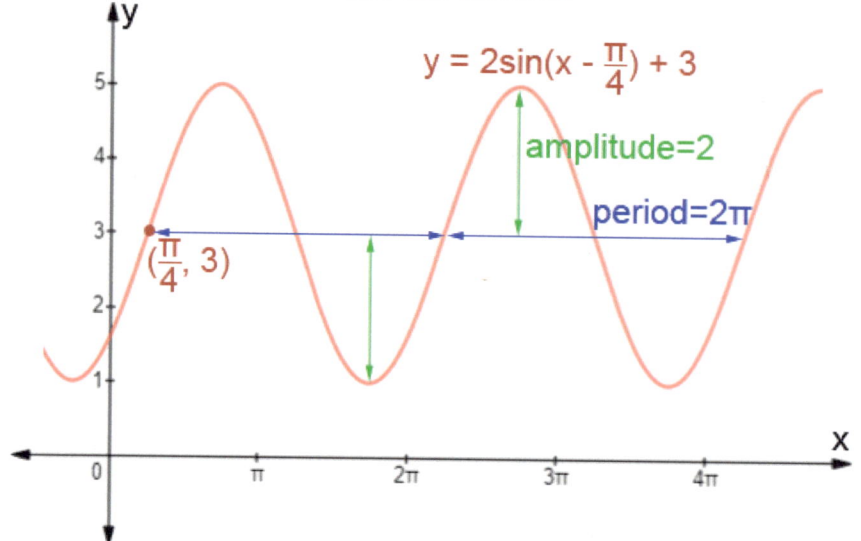

Figure 20 (3). This image is taken from math.net. The equation of the graph is given above, and the amplitude and period are labeled. The midline of this function is at $y = 3$, which makes sense visually, as that line would be at the middle of the graph.

## Practice Problems

*All 3 of the following questions are to be done without the use of a graphing calculator*

1. Consider the function $h(x) = -\frac{1}{2}\sin(2x - \pi)$. What is the domain of the function h?

   a. $[0, 2\pi]$

   b. $[\frac{\pi}{2}, \frac{3\pi}{2}]$

   c. $(-\frac{\pi}{2}, \frac{5\pi}{2})$

   d. $(-\infty, \infty)$

2. Given the function $g(x) = 4\cos(\frac{\pi}{2}x + \frac{\pi}{3})$, what is the amplitude, period, midline, and range of the function $g$?

   a. Amplitude: 4, Period: 4, Midline: $y = 0$, Range: [-4, 4]

   b. Amplitude: 4, Period: $4\pi$, Midline: $y = 0$, Range: [-4, 4]

   c. Amplitude: $\frac{1}{4}$, Period: $\frac{1}{2}$, Midline: $y = 0$, Range: $[-\frac{1}{4}, \frac{1}{4}]$

    d. Amplitude: $\frac{1}{4}$, Period: $\frac{1}{2}\pi$, Midline: $y = 0$, Range: $[-\frac{1}{4}, \frac{1}{4}]$

3. Consider the function $f(x) = sinx$. This function $f$ was horizontally compressed by a factor of 3, shifted right $\frac{\pi}{4}$, and vertically stretched by a factor of 2 to produce the function $g(x)$. Which of the following gives the correct equation for $g(x)$?

    a. $g(x) = \frac{1}{2}\sin(3x - \frac{\pi}{4})$

    b. $g(x) = 2\sin(\frac{1}{3}x - \frac{\pi}{4})$

    c. $g(x) = 2\sin(3x - \frac{\pi}{4})$

    d. $g(x) = 2\sin(3x - \frac{3\pi}{4})$

## Solutions

1. In this question we are asked to find the domain of this transformed sine function. However, if we reference the transformations discussed throughout this module, it becomes clear that none of them alter the domain of the function. Thus, the domain of this transformed function is the same as the normal sine function, that being all real numbers. Therefore, choice d is the correct answer.

2. In this question, we are asked to find the amplitude, period, midline, and range of the function. The amplitude is given by the absolute value of the $a$ value of the function, which in this case is 4. The period is found by dividing $2\pi$ by the $b$ value of the function, which in this case is $\frac{\pi}{2}$, giving us a period of 4. The midline is found through the d value of the function, which in this case is 0, and thus the midline is at $y = 0$. Finally, the range is found by adding and subtracting the amplitude to the midline, giving us a range of [-4, 4]. The only answer choice that matches all four of these traits is choice a, and thus a is the correct answer.

3. In this question, we are asked to find the function based on the transformations. To do this, let us reference our template of $f(\theta) = a\sin(b(\theta + c)) + d$. We are told that the function is horizontally compressed by a factor of 3, meaning that our $b$ value is 3. Also, it is said that the function is shifted right by $\frac{\pi}{4}$, which means our c value is $-\frac{\pi}{4}$, and remember, this goes inside the parenthesis. Finally, a vertical stretch by a factor of 2 means our $a$ value is 2. Combining all these factors together gets us $g(x) = 2\sin(3x - \frac{3\pi}{4})$. Thus, d is the correct answer. c is not the correct answer because it does properly multiply the 3 from the b value onto the c value to get $-\frac{3\pi}{4}$, and instead it uses $-\frac{\pi}{4}$.

# Module 11: Tangent Functions, Inverse and Reciprocal Trigonometric Functions

For the other trigonometric functions that don't follow a sinusoidal pattern, the first that we will start with is the tangent function. The tangent function, $f(\theta) = \tan \theta$, gives the slope of the terminal ray for the angle $\theta$ in standard position. By extension, $\tan \theta = \frac{\sin \theta}{\cos \theta}$, as $\sin \theta$ gives the $y$-value and $\cos \theta$ gives the $x$-value for the point $P$ created by the terminal ray of the angle $\theta$ in standard position. Similar to sine and cosine, tangent does demonstrate periodicity: it has a period of $\pi$. This should make sense, as every $\pi$ radians, the slope of the terminal ray repeats, and because every $\pi$ radians, both the sine and cosine are multiplied by $-1$ from their previous value. A key distinction of the tangent function, however, is its asymptotes. For the function $f(\theta) = \tan \theta$, vertical asymptotes are present for $\theta = \frac{\pi}{2} + k\pi$, where $k$ is any integer. This should make sense, as at $\theta = \frac{\pi}{2}$, $\cos \theta$ is 0, and because tangent has a period every $\pi$ radians, that means that all $\theta$ values an integer number of $\pi$ radians away from $\frac{\pi}{2}$ will have $\cos \theta$ as 0, which makes the tangent value undefined.

The general form of a tangent function is $f(\theta) = a \tan\big(b(\theta + c)\big) + d$. This is very similar to the sine and cosine equations, and thus it is easy to remember what each of these letters represents. For starters, $a$ represents a vertical dilation of the graph by $|a|$, and if $a$ is negative, then the function is reflected over the $x$-axis. Horizontal dilations are represented by $b$, which causes the period to change by $\left|\frac{1}{b}\right|$, and if $b$ is negative, then the function is reflected over the y-axis. The $c$ value represents a horizontal translation/phase shift by $-c$ units. Finally, $d$ represents a vertical translation by d units.

The next functions are the inverse trigonometric functions, which are called arcsine, arccosine, and arctangent, shortened down to arcsin, arccos, and arctan, and sometimes represented as $\sin^{-1} x$, $\cos^{-1} x$, and $\tan^{-1} x$. In these functions, the input is the coordinate value or slope that corresponds to $\theta$, while the output value for all 3 functions is $\theta$. Because trigonometric functions are periodic, however, the domains of these functions must be restricted for them to remain as functions. Specifically, the domain of arcsine is $\left[-\frac{\pi}{2},\frac{\pi}{2}\right]$, the domain of arccosine $[0,\pi]$ and the domain of arctangent is $\left(-\frac{\pi}{2},\frac{\pi}{2}\right)$.

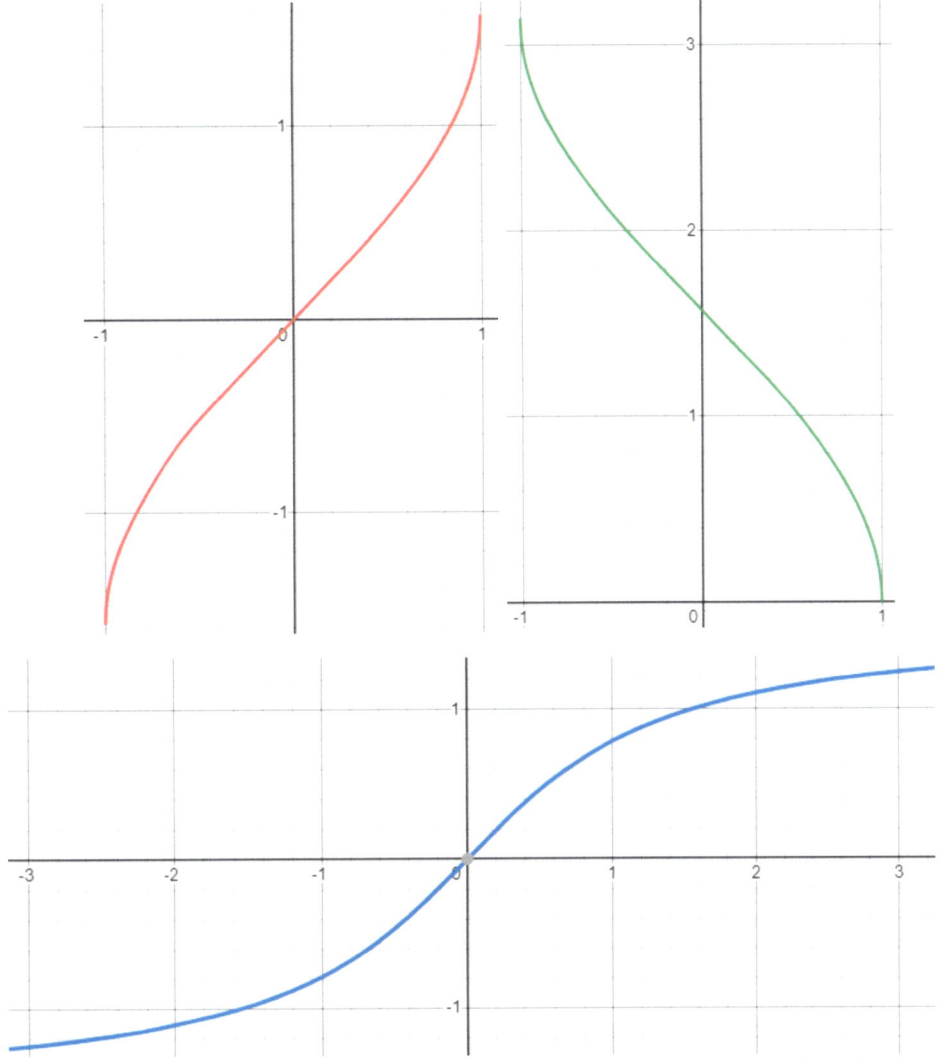

Figures 21 (1), 22 (1), and 23(1). The graphs above were made on Desmos.com. The graph on the top left with the red curve is the graph of $y = \arcsin x$. The graph on the top right with the green curve is the graph of $y = \arccos x$. The graph on the bottom with the blue curve is of the graph $y = \arctan x$. Note that while the images above for $\arcsin x$ and $\arccos x$ display the whole graph, the image for $\arctan x$ is only a section of the full graph, because the full graph approaches positive and negative infinity in the $x$ axis, though the $y$-values approach only positive and negative $\pi/2$.

Now that we covered inverse trigonometric functions, we can discuss the reciprocals. The secant function is $f(\theta) = \sec\theta$, and is the same thing as $f(\theta) = \frac{1}{\cos\theta}$. The cosecant function is $f(\theta) = \csc\theta$ and is equivalent to $f(\theta) = \frac{1}{\sin\theta}$. Thus, secant is the reciprocal of cosine while cosecant is the reciprocal of sine. For both functions, the denominator cannot be zero, and thus these reciprocal functions have vertical asymptotes where cosine and sine, respectively, are equal to zero. The range for these functions is $(-\infty, -1] \cup [1, \infty)$, as both cosine and sine cannot get larger or smaller than $-1$, and thus their reciprocals' absolute values cannot be smaller than those of the original functions. The cotangent function, $f(\theta) = \cot\theta$, is the reciprocal of the tangent function, and thus $\cot\theta = \dfrac{\cos\theta}{\sin\theta} = \dfrac{1}{\tan\theta}$. This means that for input values where sine or tangent are equal to zero, cotangent has vertical asymptotes. These can be found at $\theta = k\pi$.

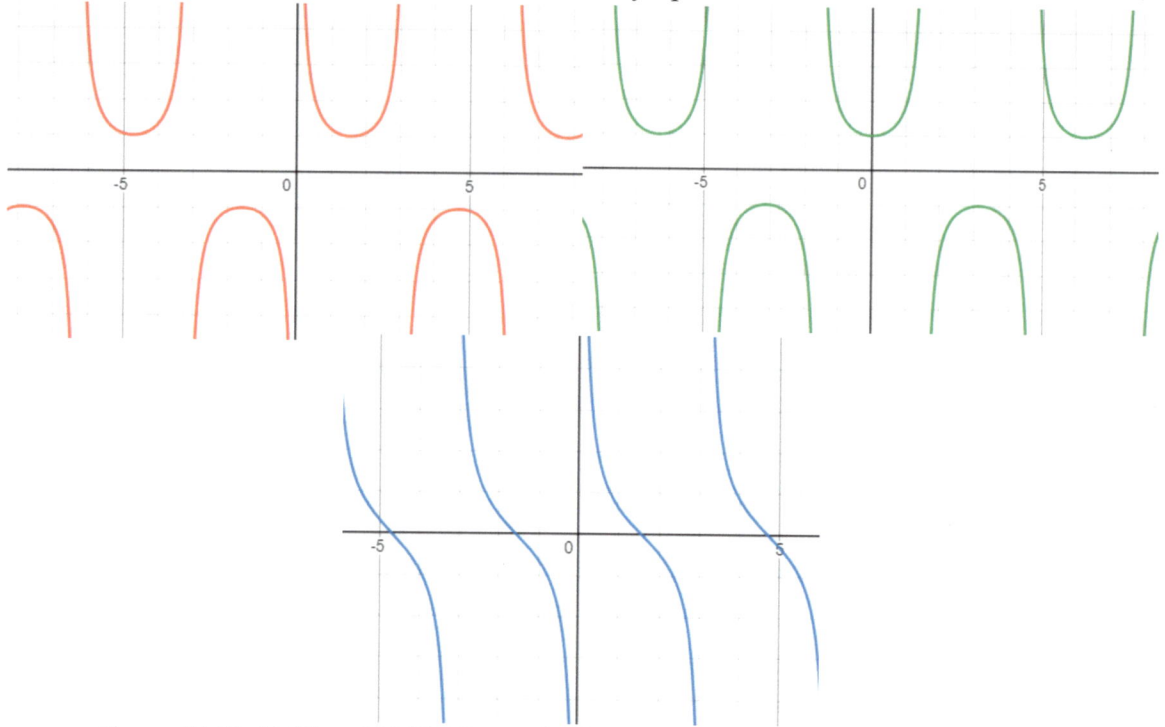

Figures 24 (1), 25 (1), and 26 (1). The graphs above were taken from Desmos.com. The graph on the top left with the red curves is the graph of $y = \csc x$, the graph on the top right with the green curves is the graph of $y = \sec x$, and the graph on the bottom with the blue curves is the graph of $y = \cot x$. All three of these graphs have $y$ values that approach positive and negative infinity, and thus these images are only sections of the graph.

## Practice Problems

*All 3 of the following questions are to be done without the use of a graphing calculator*

1. Consider the function $k(x) = -3\tan(2x - 5) + 4$, which was transformed from the parent function $f(x) = \tan x$. Which of the following lists the transformations for the function?

   a. The function is horizontally compressed by a factor of 2, shifted 5 units to the right, shifted up 4, and vertically stretched by a factor of 3.

   b. The function is horizontally compressed by a factor of 2, shifted 2.5 units to the right, shifted up 4, and vertically stretched by a factor of 3.

   c. The function is horizontally compressed by a factor of 2, shifted 2.5 units to the right, shifted up 4, vertically stretched by a factor of 3, and reflected across the x axis.

    d. The function is horizontally compressed by a factor of 2, shifted 5 units to the right, shifted up 4, vertically stretched by a factor of 3, and reflected across the x axis.

2. Consider the equation $\sin^{-1} x + \cos^{-1} x = \frac{\pi}{2}$. What value of x <u>doesn't</u> satisfy this equation?

    a. 0

    b. $\frac{\pi}{3}$

    c. $\frac{\sqrt{3}}{2}$

    d. 1

3. If $\csc\theta = -\frac{5}{3}$ and $\cos\theta > 0$, find the value of $\cot\theta$.

    a. $\frac{-3}{4}$

    b. $\frac{-3}{5}$

    c. $\frac{4}{3}$

    d. $\frac{-4}{3}$

# Solutions

1. To analyze the shifts in this function, we can use the general form of a tangent function, which is $f(\theta) = a\tan(b(\theta + c)) + d$. Our a value is -3, meaning that the function is stretched vertically by a factor of 3 and it is reflected across the x axis. Our b value is 2, while our c value is -2.5, meaning that the function is horizontally compressed by a factor of 2 and shifted to the right by 2.5. Finally, the d value is 4, meaning that the function was shifted up by 4 units. The answer choice that satisfies all these conditions is C, and thus C is the correct answer.

2. In this question, we are dealing with inverse trigonometric functions, meaning that our input should be coordinate values and our output should be angle measures. If x is 0, then $\sin^{-1} x = 0$ and $\cos^{-1} x = \frac{\pi}{2}$, and thus $\sin^{-1} x + \cos^{-1} x = \frac{\pi}{2}$, meaning choice A is incorrect. If x is $\frac{\sqrt{3}}{2}$, $\sin^{-1} x = \frac{\pi}{3}$ and $\cos^{-1} x = \frac{\pi}{6}$, meaning that $\sin^{-1} x + \cos^{-1} x = \frac{\pi}{2}$, so that means this answer is incorrect. If x is 1, $\sin^{-1} x = \pi/2$ and $\cos^{-1} x = 0$, meaning that $\sin^{-1} x + \cos^{-1} x = \pi/2$, allowing us to eliminate choice D. Thus, answer choice B is the correct option. To confirm, let's check it. Choice B

uses the angle $\frac{\pi}{3}$, which is outside the domain of both $\arcsin x$ and $\arccos x$, meaning that the sum will be undefined. Note that had the input been $\frac{\pi}{4}$, then none of the answers would've been correct, as so long as the input is the same for both $\arcsin x$ and $\arccos x$ and the input value is within the domain of both functions, then the sum will be $\frac{\pi}{2}$. This is explained by the property $\sin\theta = \cos\frac{\pi}{2} - \theta$, and because $\arcsin x = \theta$, the expression $\sin^{-1} x + \cos^{-1} x$ becomes $\theta + \left(\frac{\pi}{2} - \theta\right) = \frac{\pi}{2}$.

3. This question may seem tricky at first, but all that is being done is forming a triangle in the coordinate plane. Because $\csc\theta = -\frac{5}{3}$, $\sin\theta = -\frac{3}{5}$, meaning that we have a $y$ coordinate of $-3$ and a hypotenuse of length 5. We are told that $\cos\theta > 0$, and the only positive number that completes this triangle is 4, which you should know from the 3-4-5 right triangle. This means that our cosine value is $\frac{4}{5}$, and thus we can divide our cosine value by our sine value to find the cotangent value of $\frac{-4}{3}$. Thus, option D is the correct answer.

# Module 12: Simplifying and Solving Trigonometric Equations

Our next module revolves around trigonometric equations. In simplifying, we convert the initial equation into a different form, while solving is done to find out an angle or length that satisfies given conditions. To do this, we use trigonometric identities. There are many different identities, most of which can be derived from a few basic ones, but the following table gives of the most common ones.

| Pythagorean Identities | $\sin^2\theta + \cos^2\theta = 1$ | $1 + \tan^2\theta = \sec^2\theta$ | $1 + \cot^2\theta = \csc^2\theta$ |
|---|---|---|---|
| Cofunction Identities | $\sin\left(\frac{\pi}{2} - \theta\right) = \cos\theta$ | $\csc\left(\frac{\pi}{2} - \theta\right) = \sec\theta$ | $\tan\left(\frac{\pi}{2} - \theta\right) = \cot\theta$ |
| | $\cos\left(\frac{\pi}{2} - \theta\right) = \sin\theta$ | $\sec\left(\frac{\pi}{2} - \theta\right) = \csc\theta$ | $\cot\left(\frac{\pi}{2} - \theta\right) = \tan\theta$ |
| Even/Odd Identities | $\sin(-\theta) = -\sin\theta$ | $\cos(-\theta) = \cos\theta$ | $\tan(-\theta) = -\tan\theta$ |
| | $\csc(-\theta) = -\csc\theta$ | $\sec(-\theta) = \sec\theta$ | $\cot(-\theta) = \cot\theta$ |

| | |
|---|---|
| $\sin(a + b) = \sin a \cos b + \cos a \sin b$ | $\sin(a - b) = \sin a \cos b - \cos a \sin b$ |
| $\cos(a + b) = \cos a \cos b - \sin a \sin b$ | $\cos(a - b) = \cos a \cos b + \sin a \sin b$ |
| $\tan(a + b) = \dfrac{\tan a + \tan b}{1 - \tan a \tan b}$ | $\tan(a - b) = \dfrac{\tan a - \tan b}{1 + \tan a \tan b}$ |

The identities above can be algebraically manipulated to solve and simplify equations. For instance, the Pythagorean identities are all the same identities, just the one involving tangent and secant is the sine and cosine equation divided by cosine squared, and the one involving cotangent and cosecant is the sine and cosine equation divided by sine squared. Similarly, if you have a double angle, such as $\sin 2\theta$, you can use the sum identity of sine to split this up by setting $a$ and $b$ to both be equal to $\theta$. Let's use identities to prove $\sin^4\theta - \cos^4\theta = 1 - 2\cos^2\theta$.

$$\sin^4\theta - \cos^4\theta = 1 - 2\cos^2\theta$$

$$(\sin^2\theta + \cos^2\theta)(\sin^2\theta - \cos^2\theta) = 1 - 2\cos^2\theta$$

$$\sin^2\theta - \cos^2\theta = 1 - 2\cos^2\theta$$

$$(1 - \cos^2\theta) - \cos^2\theta = 1 - 2\cos^2\theta$$

$$1 - 2\cos^2\theta = 1 - 2\cos^2\theta$$

Note that when we simplify these equations, we must keep one side the same and only change the other side. For an example involving inverse trigonometry, here is a relatively complex example proving that $\cos^{-1} x = \sin^{-1} \sqrt{1 - x^2}$, given $\cos y = x$.

$$\cos^{-1} x = \sin^{-1} \sqrt{1 - x^2}$$

$$y = \sin^{-1} \sqrt{1 - x^2}$$

$$\sin^{-1}(\sin y) = \sin^{-1} \sqrt{1 - x^2}$$

$$\sin^{-1} \sqrt{\sin^2 y} = \sin^{-1} \sqrt{1 - x^2}$$

$$\sin^{-1} \sqrt{1 - \cos^2 y} = \sin^{-1} \sqrt{1 - x^2}$$

$$\sin^{-1} \sqrt{1 - x^2} = \sin^{-1} \sqrt{1 - x^2}$$

Note that this is restricted to the domain $[0, 1]$. The reason is that in between, when we use the variable $y$ to represent the outputs of the arccosine and arcsine functions, there are certain outputs of arccosine that don't appear in arcsine, and vice versa. The common range between arccosine and arcsine is $[0, \frac{\pi}{2}]$, which corresponds to a domain of $[0, 1]$ for both functions, and thus the domain for which the aforementioned equality remains true is $[0, 1]$. Let's try another example that uses the sum identities, but this time we will be solving rather than simplifying: $\sin\left(\frac{\pi}{6} + x\right) + \sin\left(\frac{\pi}{6} - x\right) = \frac{1}{2}$ on the interval $[0, 2\pi]$.

$$\sin\left(\frac{\pi}{6} + x\right) + \sin\left(\frac{\pi}{6} - x\right) = \frac{1}{2}$$

$$\sin\frac{\pi}{6}\cos x + \sin x \cos\frac{\pi}{6} + \sin\frac{\pi}{6}\cos -x + \sin -x \cos\frac{\pi}{6} = \frac{1}{2}$$

$$\sin\frac{\pi}{6}\cos x + \sin x \cos\frac{\pi}{6} + \sin\frac{\pi}{6}\cos x - \sin x \cos\frac{\pi}{6} = \frac{1}{2}$$

$$\sin\frac{\pi}{6}\cos x + \sin\frac{\pi}{6}\cos x = \frac{1}{2}$$

$$2\sin\frac{\pi}{6}\cos x = \frac{1}{2}$$

$$2\left(\frac{1}{2}\right)\cos x = \frac{1}{2}$$

$$\cos x = \frac{1}{2}$$

$$x = \frac{\pi}{3}, \frac{5\pi}{3}$$

Thus, from the interval of $[0, 2\pi]$, the values of $x$ that make the initial equation true are $\frac{\pi}{3}$ and $\frac{5\pi}{3}$. When solving equations like these or simplifying as we did earlier, it often requires creativity. Some general tips to help come up with a solution are to convert all the trigonometric functions into sine and cosine, to reduce the power of everything to 1 (or look for a Pythagorean identity), and if you are simplifying, then thinking of going from the end to the beginning might help. Also, whenever solving equations, make sure to take note of the domain that you are solving within and restrict your solution if necessary.

## Practice Problems

*All 3 of the following questions are to be done without the use of a graphing calculator*

1. Solve the following equation on the interval $[0, 2\pi)$: $2\sin^2 x = 1 - \cos x$.

   a. $x = \frac{2\pi}{3}, \frac{4\pi}{3}$

   b. $x = 0, 2\pi$

   c. $x = 0, \frac{2\pi}{3}, \frac{4\pi}{3}$

   d. $x = 0, \frac{2\pi}{3}, \frac{4\pi}{3}, 2\pi$

2. Which of the following is equal to $\frac{\tan x}{1+\sec x} + \frac{1+\sec x}{\tan x}$?

   a. $2\sec x$

   b. $2\csc x$

   c. $2\cos x$

   d. $2\sin x$

3. Which of the following is an equivalent form of $\frac{1-2\cos^2 x}{\sin x \cos x}$?

   a. $\sin x - \csc x$

   b. $\cos x - \sec x$

   c. $\cot x - \tan x$

   d. $\tan x - \cot x$

## Solutions

1. $2\sin^2 x = 1 - \cos x$

   $2(1 - \cos^2 x) = 1 - \cos x$

   $2 - 2\cos^2 x = 1 - \cos x$

   $0 = 2\cos^2 x - \cos x - 1$

   $0 = 2\cos^2 x - 2\cos x + \cos x - 1$

   $0 = (\cos x - 1)(2\cos x + 1)$

   $\cos x = 1, x = 0; \ 2\cos x = -1, \cos x = \dfrac{2\pi}{3}, \dfrac{4\pi}{3}$

   Thus, the correct answer choice is C. D is incorrect because $2\pi$ is not included in the solution interval.

2. $\dfrac{\tan x}{1+\sec x} + \dfrac{1+\sec x}{\tan x}$

   $\dfrac{\frac{\sin x}{\cos x}}{\frac{\cos x}{\cos x}+\frac{1}{\cos x}} + \dfrac{\frac{\cos x}{\cos x}+\frac{1}{\cos x}}{\frac{\sin x}{\cos x}}$

   $\dfrac{\sin x}{\cos x + 1} + \dfrac{\cos x + 1}{\sin x}$

   $\dfrac{\sin^2 x}{\sin x \cos x + \sin x} + \dfrac{\cos^2 x + 2\cos x + 1}{\sin x \cos x + \sin x}$

   $\dfrac{\sin^2 x + \cos^2 x + 2\cos x + 1}{\sin x \cos x + \sin x}$

   $\dfrac{1 + 2\cos x + 1}{\sin x \cos x + \sin x}$

   $\dfrac{2(\cos x + 1)}{\sin x(\cos x + 1)}$

   $\dfrac{2}{\sin x} = 2\csc x$

   Thus, B is the correct answer

3. $\dfrac{1-2\cos^2 x}{\sin x \cos x}$

   $\dfrac{1 - \cos^2 x - \cos^2 x}{\sin x \cos x}$

$$\frac{\sin^2 x - \cos^2 x}{\sin x \cos x}$$

$$\frac{\sin^2 x}{\sin x \cos x} - \frac{\cos^2 x}{\sin x \cos x}$$

$$\frac{\sin x}{\cos x} - \frac{\cos x}{\sin x}$$

$$\tan x - \cot x$$

Thus, the correct answer is D.

# Module 13: Polar Functions

To go along with our discussion of trigonometry, we can discuss a new coordinate system: polar coordinates. As opposed to rectangular coordinates, which are in the form $(x, y)$, polar coordinates are in the form $(r, \theta)$, wherein $r$ is the radius of the circle that the point lies on and $\theta$ is the measure of the standard position angle that creates the terminal ray on which the point lies. To convert this into the rectangular coordinate system, we use the equations $x = r \cos \theta$ and $y = r \sin \theta$. Thus, the point $(2, \frac{\pi}{4})$ converts to $(\sqrt{2}, \sqrt{2})$. To convert back from rectangular coordinates into polar coordinates, we use the equations $r = \sqrt{x^2 + y^2}$ and $\theta = \tan^{-1}\left(\frac{y}{x}\right)$ for when $x > 0$. If $x$ is negative, then we add $\pi$ to the angle, because if we don't add $\pi$, the arctan function will return an angle in the first or fourth quadrant while the actual angle is in the second or third quadrants. Thus, if we have the point $(-3, -3)$ in the rectangular plane, it converts to the polar coordinate $(3\sqrt{2}, \frac{5\pi}{4})$. Finally, complex numbers in the form of $a + bi$ are expressed in the complex rectangular plane as $(a, b)$, but in the polar plane, they are expressed as $r \cos \theta + i(r \sin \theta)$. To understand why this is the formula, remember that $r \cos \theta = x$ and $r \sin \theta = y$. In this case, the $x$ coordinate is $a$ and our $y$ coordinate is $b$, and thus $r \cos \theta = a$ while $r \sin \theta = b$. Earlier we said that complex numbers are in the form $a + bi$, and using substitution we get $r \cos \theta + i(r \sin \theta)$.

As for polar functions, they are in the form $r = f(\theta)$, wherein the inputs are angle measures and the outputs are radii. Thus, changing domain values would be changing the angle from the $x$ axis and changing range values would be changing distance from the origin. If on a given interval, the values of $r$ are positive and increasing as $\theta$ increases, or alternatively the values of $r$ are negative and decreasing as $\theta$ increasing, then the distance between $f(\theta)$ and the origin increasing, because both of those cases means that $|r|$ is increasing. By extension, if the $r$ values are positive but decreasing or negative but increasing, then the distance between $f(\theta)$ and the origin is decreasing, because $|r|$ is decreasing. On a given interval when $r$ changes from increasing to decreasing or decreasing to increasing, extrema can be found on the points where $|r|$ are the largest or smallest, and thus the points closest to or furthest from the origin. Finally, the rate of change for these functions is calculated the same way change is normally calculated: the change in output values divided by the change in input values. Thus, the rate of change is the change in radius values divided by the change in $\theta$ values. This can be verbally stated to be the rate at which the radius changes per radian.

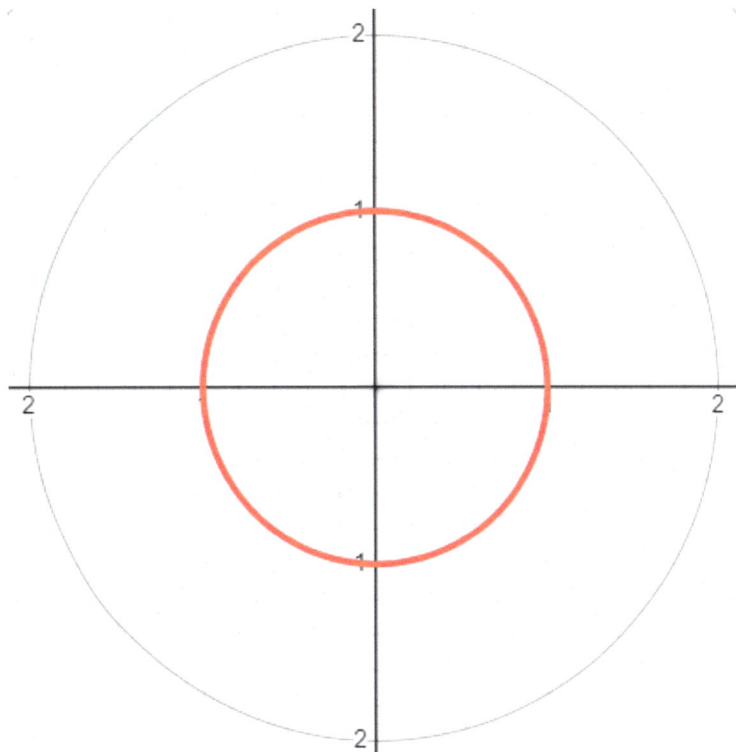

Figure 27 (1). This graph was made on Desmos.com. The graph is in the polar plane and is of the function $r = \sin\frac{\pi}{2}$. A circle is formed because $\sin\frac{\pi}{2}$ is a constant, that being 1, and just as how in the rectangular plane, when $y$ is equal to a constant a vertical line is formed, when $r$ is equal to a constant, a circle is formed. Note that if we set $\theta$ to be equal to a constant, then a line will be formed, as $r$ is not clearly defined and thus points can be any distance away from the origin so long as they are the correct angle.

To graph a point on this polar coordinate grid, we must go in the direction of the angle $\theta$ and move a distance of $r$ away from the origin in the direction of $\theta$. If the angle $\theta$ is negative, then first convert it to a positive angle by adding $2\pi$, and then accordingly go $r$ away from the origin. If the value $r$ is negative, however, then you must go in the opposite direction, meaning that you first add $\pi$ to $\theta$, and then move a distance of $|r|$ from the origin. Note that the polar grid has the polar axis rather than the $x$-axis, and rather than the $y$-axis, it has the line $\theta = \frac{\pi}{2}$.

Using this graph, we can now analyze different types of functions. First, we have circles, which are in the form $r = a \sin\theta$ or $a \cos\theta$, where $a$ is the diameter of the circle. If the circle is from sine, then it lies on the line $\theta = \frac{\pi}{2}$, but if the circle is from the cosine function, then it lies on the polar axis. If $a$ is negative, then the circle lies below the polar axis or on the left side of the line $\theta = \frac{\pi}{2}$ for $r = \sin\theta$ and $r = \cos\theta$ respectively.

Next we have limaçons. These are in the form $r = a + b \sin\theta$, where $a, b \neq 0$ and both $a$ and $b$ can be positive or negative. When $a < b$, the limaçon will have an inner loop, wherein the inner loop will extend out to $a - b$ and the outer loop will extend out to $a + b$, and the axis ($\theta = \frac{\pi}{2}$ for cosine functions and the polar axis for sine functions) is intersected at $\pm b$. Figure 28 shows the graph of a limaçon for a cosine function.

65

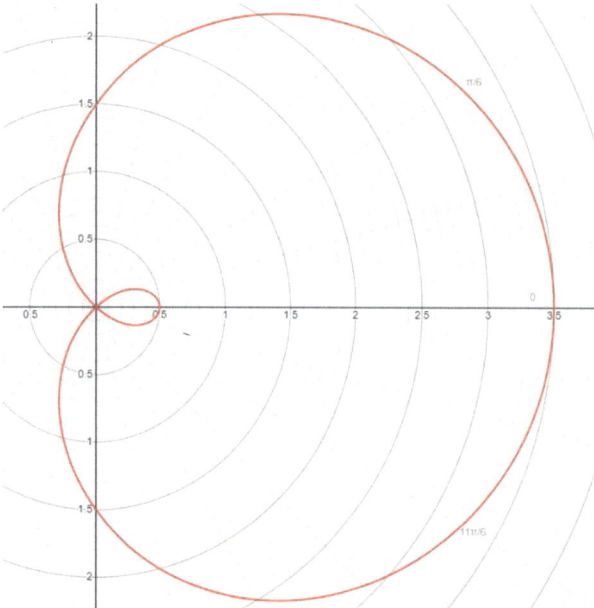

Figure 28 (1). This graph was made on Desmos.com. It is of the function $r = 1.5 + 2\cos\theta$. Notice how the outer loop extends all the way to 3.5, which is equal to $a + b$, while the inner loop reaches 0.5, which is equal to $a - b$. Finally, the line $\theta = \frac{\pi}{2}$ is intersected at 1.5 and $-1.5$, which is equal to $\pm b$.

When $a$ is equal to $b$, however, the graph loses its inner loop, and it is known as a cardioid. Apart from the loop, cardioids are the same as limaçons with the loops, in that they intersect an axis at $\pm b$ and their loop reaches out to $|a + b|$, which is equal to $2a$ in this case. However, if $b$ is negative, then the loop will extend to $-|a + b|$. These same features are also shared with dimpled limaçons, wherein $b < a < 2b$, and these appear similar to cardioids, as shown in figure 28. However, dimpled limaçons have an added feature, in that they have a loop that extends out in the opposite direction as the major loop. The size of this loop is $\left||a| - |b|\right|$.

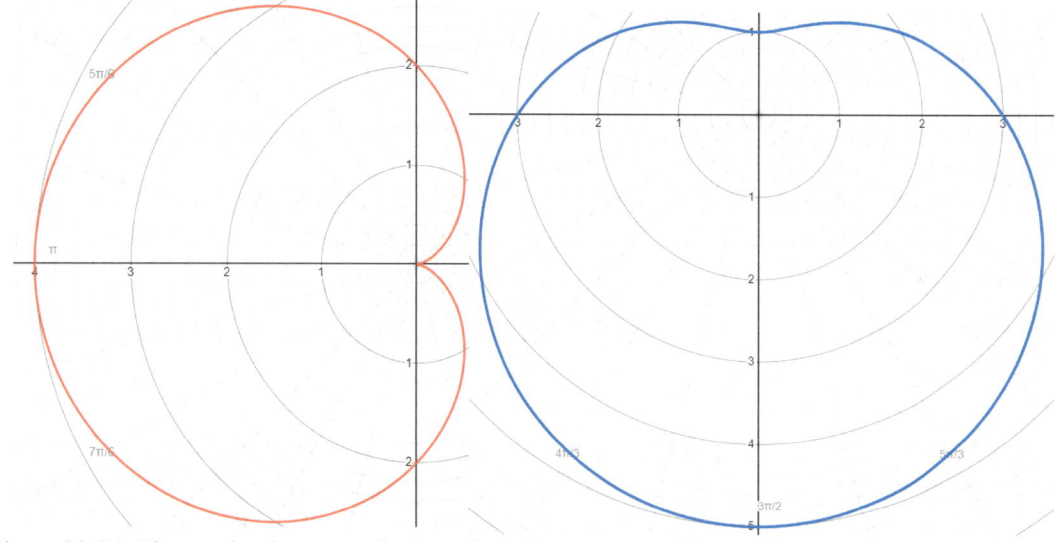

Figure 29 (1). The graphs above were both made on Desmos.com. The graph on the left in red is of the cardioid $r = -2\cos\theta + 2$, while the graph on the right is of the dimpled limaçon $r = -2\sin\theta - 3$. Notice how the major loops for both graphs reach out to $a + b$, while the inner dimple for both is at $a - b$, which is 0 in the case of the cardioid. Also, both graphs intersect an axis at $\pm b$.

The final type of limaçon is a convex limaçon, wherein $a \geq 2b$. These are essentially the same as dimpled limaçons, and are classified differently due to their $a$ value being greater than or equal to $2b$ and because rather than having a dimple, they appear more circle-like, as shown in figure 29.

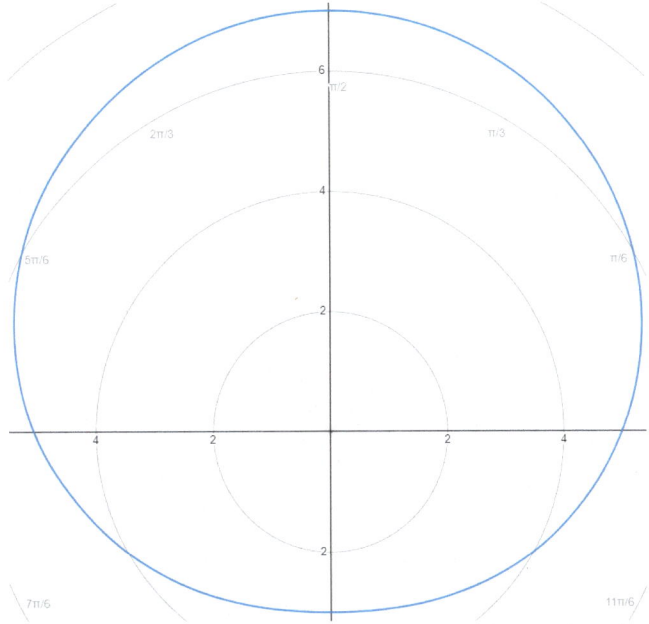

Figure 30 (1). This graph was made on Desmos.com. Similar to the previous limaçons, the graph intersects one axis at $a \pm b$ and the other axis at $\pm b$. However, unlike the other graphs, which had inner loops and dimples, this graph is more rounded at the opposite end of the major loop due to the magnitude of it's $a$ value.

The next polar function type is a rose. These are in the form $r = \cos k\theta$ or $r = \sin k\theta$, where $k$ is a nonzero real number, although almost always an integer. If $k$ is an odd integer, then the rose has $k$ petals. If $k$ is an even integer, then the rose has $2k$ petals. To determine whether a rose is sine function or cosine function, the symmetry must be analyzed. If the rose is symmetric by the line $\theta = \frac{\pi}{2}$, then it is a sine function. If it is symmetric by the polar axis, it is a cosine function. If it is symmetric by both, which is often the case with an even number of petals, then plug in values to determine which function it is. If the function is multiplied by a constant then the size of the petals increases. For instance, $r = 2\cos 3\theta$ has 3 petals with a length of 2.

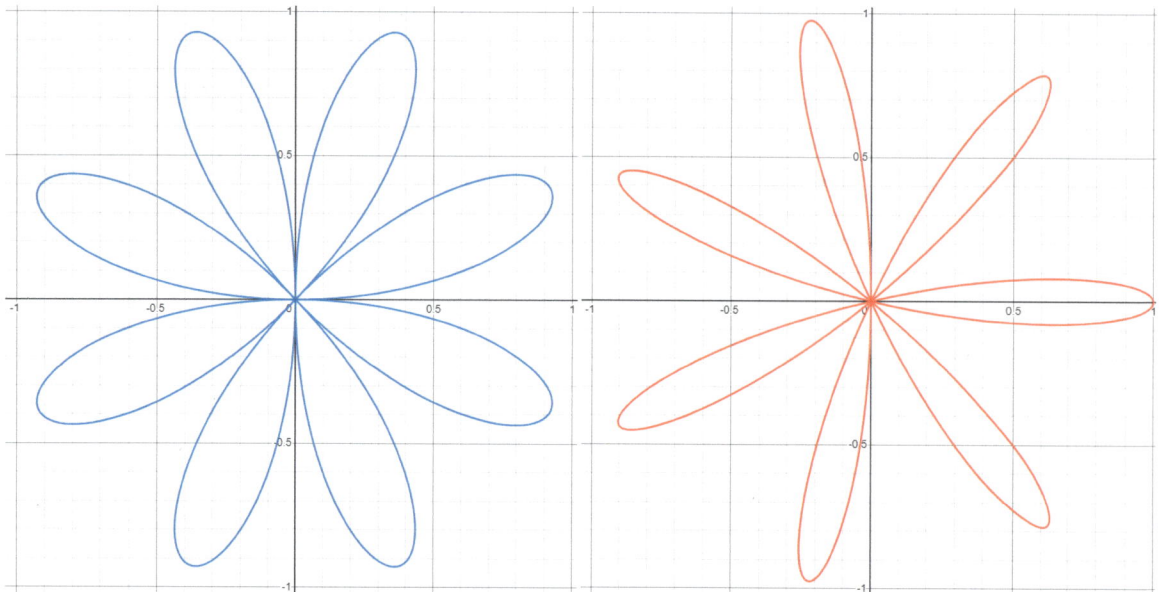

Figures 31 (1) and 32 (1). The graphs above were made on Desmos.com. The graph on the left is of the function $r = \cos 7\theta$ while the graph on the right is of the function $r = \sin 4\theta$. Notice how the graph on the left has 7 petals while the graph on the right has 8, because it has an even coefficient in front of $\theta$. Also, the cosine function is symmetric by the polar axis while the sine function has both types of symmetry. Plugging in important $\theta$ values, such as $\frac{\pi}{2}$, reveal that it is a sine function.

After that, another polar function type is a lemniscate. These are in the form $r^2 = a^2 \cos 2\theta$ or $r^2 = a^2 \sin 2\theta$, where $a$ is a nonzero constant. If it is a lemniscate based on the cosine function, then it is centered on the polar axis. If it is a lemniscate based on the sine function, then it is centered on the line $\theta = \frac{\pi}{4}$. These functions are centered on the origin, and thus adding a value in order to horizontally or vertically shift the function will not work, also in part due to the fact that these are graphed in the polar plane. The $a$ value determines how far out on the axis the lemniscate expands.

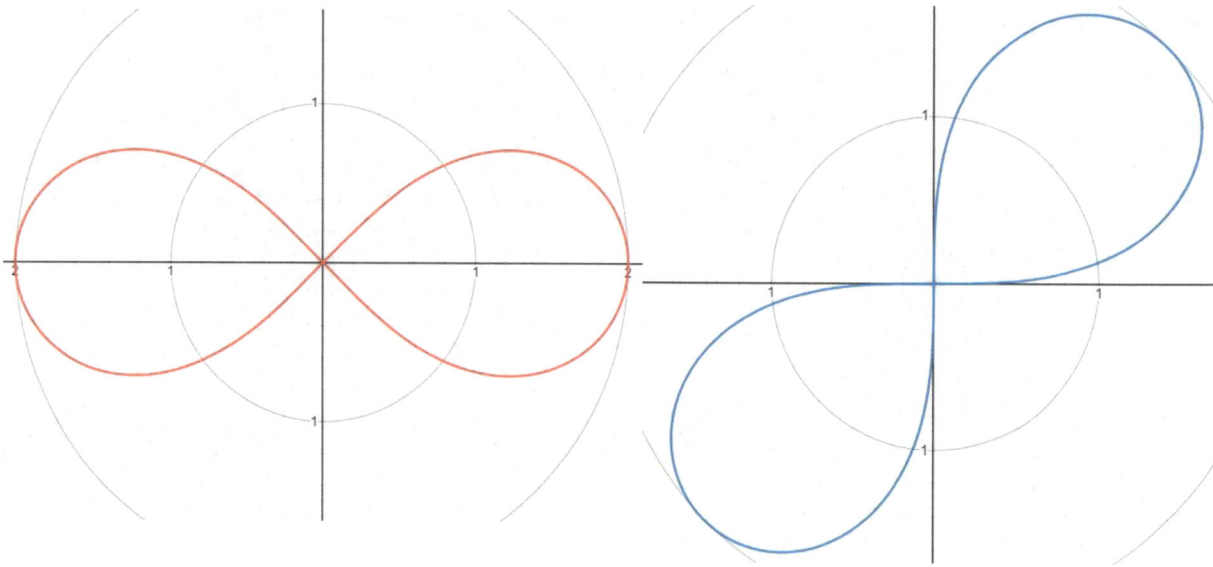

Figures 33 (1) and 34 (1). The graphs above were made on Desmos.com. The graph on the left is of the function $r^2 = 4\cos 2\theta$ while the graph on the right is of the function $r^2 = 4\sin 2\theta$. Notice how for each graph, because the $a$ value is 2, the edge of their curves reached out to a distance of 2 from the origin. Also, the cosine function is centered on the polar axis while the sine function is centered on the line $\theta = \frac{\pi}{4}$.

The final type of polar function is the spiral of Archimedes. These are in the form $r = a\theta$, where $a$ is a constant and the sign of $\theta$ determines if it opens upwards or downwards.

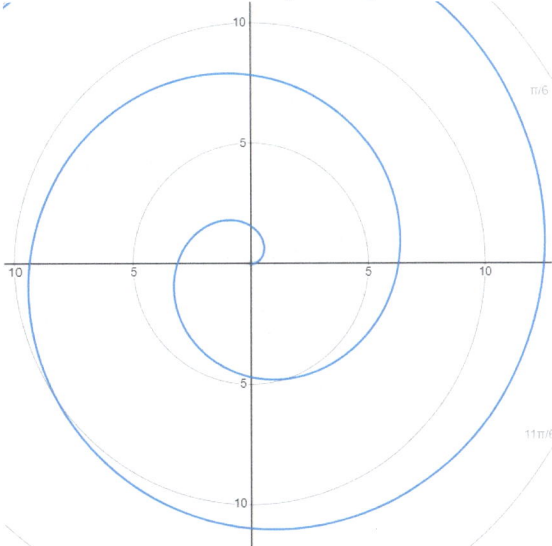

Figure 35 (1). The graph above was made on Desmos.com. It is of the function $r = \theta$. Notice how because our $a$ value of 1 is positive, the graph opens up.

A lot of functions were covered in this module, and so it is most important to remember the basics of how the polar plane works first and how coordinates are graphed, as from there you can understand how each of these functions work. Furthermore, the most commonly seen function among the aforementioned graphs is the limaçon, so be sure to familiarize yourself with the various types of them.

## Practice Problems

*A graphing calculator is permitted for all three of the following questions*

1. Given the point $\left(3, \frac{\pi}{6}\right)$ in the polar plane, which of the following gives the point in rectangular coordinates?

   a. $\left(\frac{3}{2}, \frac{3\sqrt{3}}{2}\right)$

   b. $\left(\frac{3\sqrt{3}}{2}, \frac{3}{2}\right)$

   c. $\left(-\frac{3}{2}, \frac{3\sqrt{3}}{2}\right)$

   d. $\left(\frac{3}{2}, -\frac{3\sqrt{3}}{2}\right)$

2. The limaçon $r = 2 - 4\sin\theta$ is graphed in the polar plane. Which of the following gives the coordinates of the polar axis intercepts?

   a. $(4, 0)$ and $(4, \pi)$

   b. $(4, \frac{\pi}{2})$ and $(4, \frac{3\pi}{2})$

   c. $(2, 0)$ and $(2, \pi)$

   d. $(2, \frac{\pi}{2})$ and $(2, \frac{3\pi}{2})$

3. The rose $r = 31\cos 42\theta$ is graphed in the polar plane. Which of the following gives the characteristics of the graph?

   a. The graph has 31 petals, each with a length of 42 units, and the graph is centered on the polar axis

   b. The graph has 42 petals, each with a length of 31 units, and the graph is centered on the line $\theta = \frac{\pi}{2}$

   c. The graph has 84 petals, each with a length of 31 units, and the graph is centered on the polar axis

   d. The graph has 21 petals, each with a length of 31 units, and the graph is centered on the polar axis

## Solutions

1. In this question, we are asked to find the rectangular coordinates of a polar point. To do this, we must remember that a point $(x, y)$ is the same as $(r\cos\theta, r\sin\theta)$ in the polar plane. Furthermore, polar points are given in the form $(r, \theta)$. Thus, to find the $x$ and $y$ values, we must find the according trigonometric ratio and multiply by the $r$ value. For the $x$ coordinate, $3\cos\frac{\pi}{6} = 3\left(\frac{\sqrt{3}}{2}\right) = \frac{3\sqrt{3}}{2}$. For the $y$ coordinate, $3\sin\frac{\pi}{6} = 3\left(\frac{1}{2}\right) = \frac{3}{2}$. Thus, the correct answer is B.

2. In this question, we are asked to find the polar axis intercepts of a limaçon. Recall that because this is a sine function, the polar axis intercepts are going to be at $\pm b$, where $b$ is the constant added to the sine function. In this case, our $b$ value is 2, and because we are using polar coordinates, we must use angles of 0 and $\pi$ to get 2 and $-2$. Thus, the correct answer is C.

3.  In this question, we asked to find the characteristics of the graph of a rose. Note that the standard equation for a rose is $r = a \cos b\theta$, where $a$ is the length of the petals and $b$ or $2b$ gives the number of petals, depending on if $b$ is odd or even respectively. In this case, our $a$ value is 31, so our petals are 31 units long. Our $b$ value is 42, and because this is an even number, this means we have 84 petals. Finally, because this is a cosine function, it is centered on the polar axis. Thus, the correct answer choice is option C.

# Unit 4: Parametric functions, Conic Sections, Vectors, and Matrices

- Module 14: Parametric Functions

- Module 15: Implicitly Defined Functions and Parametrization

- Module 16: Conic Sections

- Module 17: Vectors and Vector-Valued Functions

- Module 18: Matrices

# Module 14: Parametric Functions

To start off the final unit of this course, we have parametric functions. These are functions in which both $x$ and $y$ are dependent variables and $t$, the parameter, is the independent variable. Because both $x$ and $y$ are dependent on $t$, we can now define both $x$ and $y$ as functions of $t$, while also being able to define $y$ in terms of $x$ through manipulation of their $t$ functions. The set of points for a parametric function, therefore, is in the form $f(t) = (x(t), y(t))$. The parameter $t$ often is thought of as time, meaning that the parametrically defined function $f(t)$ gives the values of $x$ and $y$ at time $t$, or in other words, the coordinates $(x_i, y_i)$ are the $x$ and $y$ values of a parametric function at the time $t_i$. To graph these functions, a table of datapoints based on successive values of $t$ is made, and then these points are graphed to make the function, with arrows being drawn to indicate the direction of increasing $t$ values. Finally, because $t$ does not necessarily extend to infinity as $x$ often does but rather might only be a finite set of values, the domain and range of parametric functions may be restricted. Also, note that it is possible for curves that are defined by parametric equations to not be functions.

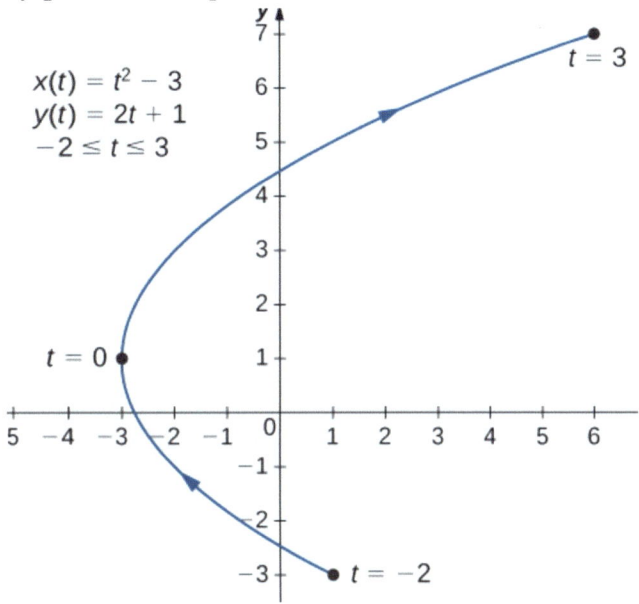

$$x(t) = t^2 - 3$$
$$y(t) = 2t + 1$$
$$-2 \leq t \leq 3$$

Figure 36 (4). This image was cropped from math.libretexts.org. In this image above, a curve is defined by the parameter $t$. Notice that these equations do not define a function. Furthermore, specific points are labeled for their $y$-values and arrows are used to display the direction of increasing values of $t$ along the curve.

A specific context in which parametric functions are often used is to define particle motion. Specifically, as time $t$ passes on, $x$ models the horizontal motion of the particle while $y$ models the vertical motion. Therefore, the extreme values of $x(t)$ give the extreme horizontal values, the extreme values of $y(t)$ give the extreme vertical values, the zeros of $x(t)$ give the $y$-intercepts, and the zeros of $y(t)$ give the $x$-intercepts. Furthermore, because $x(t)$ and $y(t)$ are separate functions, their rates of changes can be independently computed over an interval $[t_1, t_2]$, and the ratio of the average rate of change for $y$ to the average rate of change for $x$ gives the slope of the curve over the $t$ interval, as long as the change in $x$ isn't 0.

Finally, parameters can be used to define trigonometric functions. On the unit circle, a point can be defined as $(\cos\theta, \sin\theta)$, where $\cos\theta$ gives the $x$ coordinate and $\sin\theta$ gives the $y$ coordinate. Using our parameter $t$, however, we can redefine this as $(\cos t, \sin t)$ and $(x(t), y(t))$, where $0 \le t \le 2\pi$. Also, given the equations $x = 3\cos t$ and $y = 3\sin t$, we can convert this into a circle using the Pythagorean identity.

$$\cos^2 t + \sin^2 t = 1$$

$$\left(\frac{x}{3}\right)^2 + \left(\frac{y}{3}\right)^2 = 1$$

$$\frac{x^2}{9} + \frac{y^2}{9} = 1$$

$$x^2 + y^2 = 9$$

Using this example, it becomes clear that trigonometric identities can be used to simplify parametric equations that involve trigonometric equations.

## Practice Problems

*A graphing calculator is permitted for all three of the following questions.*

1. Given parametric equations $x = 2t + 4$ and $y = 3t + 6$, find the slope of the line made from these equations. Furthermore, given a minimum $x$ value of 2, find the minimum $y$ value and $t$ value.

   a. $3x; 3, 2$

   b. $2x; 1; 2$

   c. $\frac{3}{2}x; 3; -1$

   d. $\frac{3}{2}x; 2, -1$

2. Given parametric equations $x = 4t - 17$ and $y = -4x^2 + 5$, produce an equation for $y$ in terms of $t$. Furthermore, on the interval $-13 \le t \le 7$, what is the lowest $y$ value?

   a. $y = 16t^2 - 136t + 289; 4{,}761$

   b. $y = 16t^2 - 136t + 294; 4{,}765$

   c. $y = -64t^2 + 544t - 1{,}155; -3$

   d. $y = -64t^2 + 544t - 1{,}155; -19{,}039$

3. Given parametric equations $x = 12 \cos t$ and $y = 6 \sin t$, find the equation of the graph in the rectangular plane and give the domain of the graph in the rectangular plane.

    a. $x^2 + 4y^2 = 36; [-12, 12]$

    b. $x^2 + 4y^2 = 144; [-6, 6]$

    c. $\frac{x^2}{144} + \frac{y^2}{36} = 1; [-12, 12]$

    d. $\frac{x^2}{144} + \frac{y^2}{36} = 1; [-6, 6]$

## Solutions

1. In this question, we are asked to find the slope of the line made from given parametric equations and the minimum $y$ and $t$ values. To do this, we must first create an equation for $y$ based on $x$. Algebraically, we can make an equation for $t$ in terms of $x$, yielding $t = \frac{x-4}{2}$. Now, we can plug this into the equation for $y$, yielding $y = \frac{3}{2}x$. Alternatively, through observation, it can be seen that $x = 2(t + 2)$ and $y = 3(t + 2)$, and thus $y = \frac{3}{2}x$. To extract the minimum $y$ value, because these equations produce a line, we can simply plug the minimum x value into our equation, yielding 3. To find the minimum t value, the same process can be done to get a minimum t value of $-1$. Thus, the correct answer is option C.

2. In this question, we are asked to create an equation for y in terms of t and then find the lowest y value. In this case, we can directly substitute the equation for x into the equation for y. After squaring the equation $x = 4t - 17$, multiplying it by $-4$, and adding 5, we get the equation $y = -64t^2 + 544t - 1,155$. From there, using the table feature in your calculator and ensuring you are in the parametric mode, check the values of the function for the given t interval. For the t value of $-13, y = -19,039$. Thus, the correct answer choice is option D.

3. In this question, we are asked to convert parametric equations into an equation with only $x$ and $y$ and find the domain of this function. We can produce the equation used the same method discussed earlier in the chapter, using the equations $\cos t = \frac{x}{12}, \sin t = \frac{y}{6}$, and $\cos^2 t + \sin^2 t = 1$. This yields the equation $\frac{x^2}{144} + \frac{y^2}{36} = 1$, which can be converted to $x^2 + 4y^2 = 144$, although that isn't necessary in this question. To find the domain, once again use your graphing calculator and either look directly at the graph or use the table feature. The oval shape produced is known as an ellipse, which will be discussed in a future chapter. Logically, because this is a similar shape to a circle and because this is centered on the origin, the extreme values of $x$ happen when $y = 0$, and so

substitution of 0 for $y$ could also be used to yield the domain of $[-12, 12]$, meaning that C is the correct answer choice.

# Module 15: Implicitly Defined Functions and Parametrization

The next topic that is covered in this unit is implicitly defined functions and the parametrization of those functions. First, we need to discuss implicitly defined functions. Implicitly defined functions are relationships between two variables that represent one or more functions, partially or fully. These equations aren't in the same form as most other functions you have seen thus far, as those functions are on the form of one variable, $y$, in terms of another variable $x$. A good example of an implicitly defined function would be the equation of a circle:

$$x^2 + y^2 = r^2$$

From this equation we can see that both $x$ and $y$ are on the same side of the equal sign and a constant is on the other side. This is a common form that implicitly defined functions can take on; however, this is not the only form that implicitly defined functions are in. Instead, there can be variables on both sides of the equal sign. Due to this, implicitly defined functions are limitless in nature and can define a wide variety of graphs that regular functions simply cannot.

The equation we looked at earlier graphed a circle, which upon further inspection you find is not a function since circles fail the vertical line test. This brings us to the next point which is that implicitly defined functions can define graphs that aren't functions. Another good example of this is the implicit equation:

$$(y - 2)^2 - x = 3$$

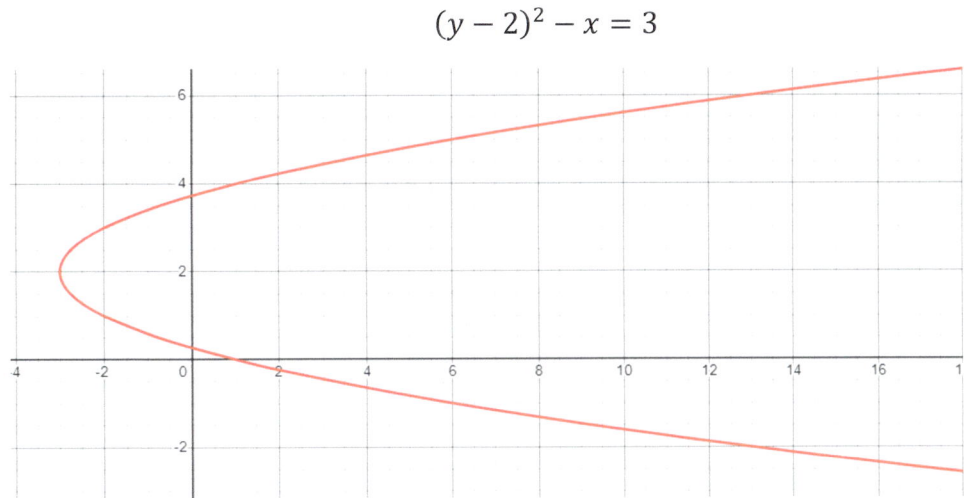

Figure 37 (1). This image was made on Desmos.com as a graph of the implicit equation $(y - 2)^2 - x = 3$.

Looking at this graph we can already tell that this isn't a function, rather is a side parabola. However, through algebraic manipulation, we can convert the equation into a more familiar form, and even create two functions. Let's start off with the easier variable to solve for in this equation, $x$.

$$(y - 2)^2 = x + 3$$

$$y^2 - 4y + 4 = x + 3$$

$$x = y^2 - 4y + 1$$

This is not a function. Solving for $y$, shown below, similarly doesn't produce a function.

$$(y - 2)^2 = x + 3$$

$$y - 2 = \pm\sqrt{x + 3}$$

$$y = 2 \pm \sqrt{x + 3}$$

Both equations produce the same graph and neither of them are functions because the graph fails the vertical line test. However, it is possible to turn the second equation into two different functions. This is done by considering both positive and negative parts of the equation as separate functions.

$$y = 2 + \sqrt{x + 3}$$

$$y = 2 - \sqrt{x + 3}$$

These two functions produce the graphs below.

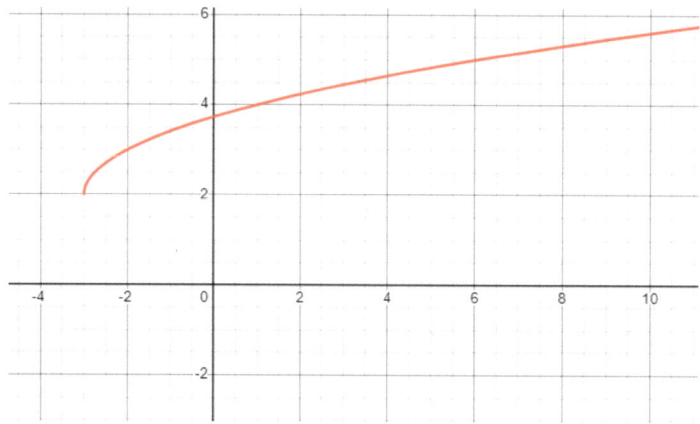

Figure 38 (1). This image was made on Desmos.com. This is the graph of the function $y = \sqrt{x + 3} + 2$

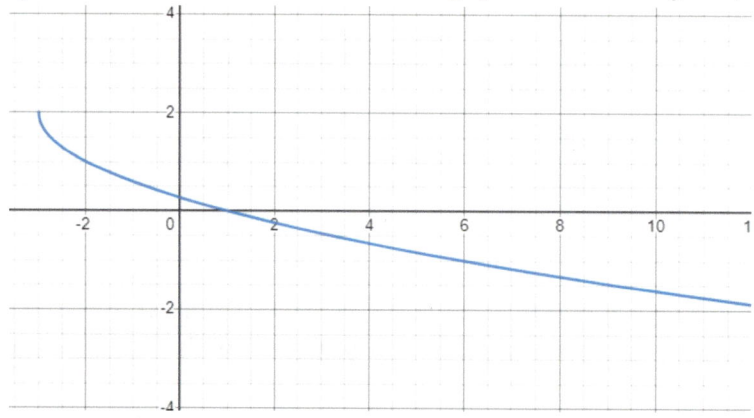

Figure 39 (1). This image was made on Desmos.com. This is the graph of the function $y = -\sqrt{x + 3} + 2$

A couple things to note from these graphs is that these two graphs are different parts of the graph of

$$(y - 2)^2 - x = 3$$

The next thing we look at in this topic is the rate of change of one variable with respect to another. To have a better look at this we can solve the implicit equation to where it is in the form of one variable in terms of another. In the previous equation we saw that when we solved for $x$, we saw that there was a quadratic relationship between $x$ and $y$ within that form while then when we solved for $y$ we saw that there a square root relationship between $x$ and $y$. This bring us to the next point, which is that in implicitly defined functions, $x$ and $y$ have different rates of change and that the rate of change of one variable can be zero while the other is nonzero or both rates of change can be zero. In cases where the rate of change of $y$ is zero the tangent line at the point, or the entire interval, will be horizontal. In cases where the rate of change of $x$ is zero the tangent line, or entire interval, will be a vertical, and in cases where the rates of change of both $x$ and $y$ are zero, a corner or cusp is usually formed at those points.

In the previous lesson we learned that parametric equations are functions to where both $x$ and $y$ are dependent on a variable $t$. For example, if $f$ is a function of $x$, and $x$ can be defined by the parameter $t$, the function $f(x)$ can be defined as $(x(t), y(t))$ and $(t, f(t))$. Using this property, we can substitute the parameter $t$ in for $x$ and $y$ and have the function $f$ defined by t. This allows for the simplification of implicit equations as this allows us to replace the $x$'s and $y$'s with $t$ allowing the equation to be in terms of one variable. To show this let's take the implicit equation for a circle with any radius:

$$(x - h)^2 + (y - k)^2 = r^2$$

The first thing to consider when converting a function into parametric form is what the variable $t$ will represent. The first thing to note about this equation is that $(h, k)$ is the center of this circle and all points on the circle are an equal distance $r$ away from that point. Now let's consider a point on the circle $(x, y)$. As we have established before we know that this point is a distance $r$ away from the center of the circle, but now that we have the point $(x, y)$ we are able to find the horizontal distance from the center by subtracting the $x$-coordinate of the center, $h$, from the $x$-coordinate of the given point, $x$, to get $(x - h)$. Doing the same with the $y$-coordinates yields $(y - k)$. Using these values, we can create a right triangle within the circle with $r$ as the hypotenuse. By forming this triangle, we have created a right triangle, which allows us to use right triangle trigonometry

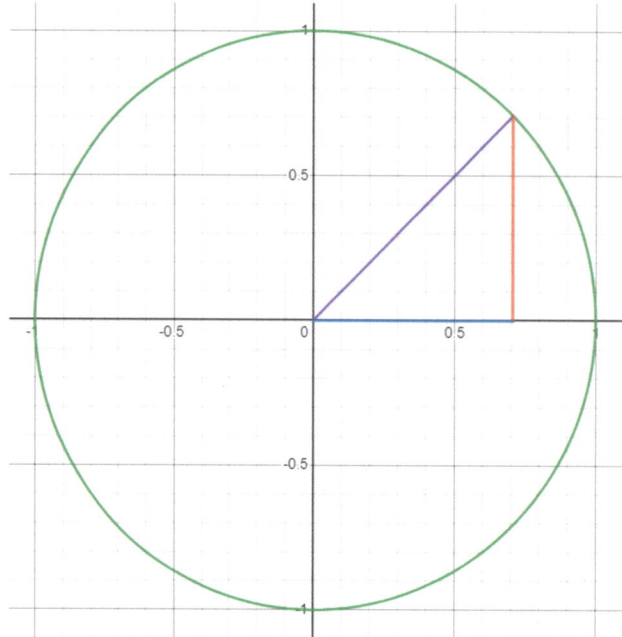

Figure 40 (1). This image was made on Desmos.com. This is the graph of a circle with radius 1. The purple line represents the radius $r$, the blue line represents the horizontal distance from the center $x - h$, and the red line represents the vertical distance from the center $y - k$. The point at which these three lines intersect on the circle is $(x - h, y - k)$.

Now we can determine a value for $t$. Because we have a right triangle, we can use the angle formed at $(h, k)$ as our parameter $t$. Using right triangle trigonometry, we can determine the following:

$$sin(t) = \frac{y - k}{r}$$
$$cos(t) = \frac{x - h}{r}$$

Rearranging these two equations in to get $x$ and $y$ in terms of $t$ we get:

$$x(t) = rcos(t) + h$$
$$y(t) = rsin(t) + k$$

Then we can plug in both formulas into the original equation, getting us:

$$(h + rcos(t) - h)^2 + (k + rsin(t) - k)^2 = r^2.$$

From these we can cancel out the $h$ and $k$ terms and square the values in the parentheses and be left with equation

$$r^2cos^2(t) + r^2sin^2(t) = r^2$$

From here we can divide both sides by $r^2$ leaving us with the equation

$$cos^2(t) + sin^2(t) = 1$$

This is one the Pythagorean identities. The next two equations we will parametrize will be the equations for an ellipse and a hyperbola. Both ellipses and hyperbolas are conic sections, something that is going to be discussed further in the next module. First let's parametrize the equation for an ellipse:

$$\frac{(x-h)^2}{a^2} + \frac{(y-k)^2}{b^2} = 1$$

The first thing to notice about this equation is the resemblance it has to the equation of a circle, and because of this we can use the Pythagorean identity

$$cos^2(t) + sin^2(t) = 1$$

As we learned in our previous unit on trigonometry, $x$ corresponds to cosine and $y$ corresponds to sine. This results in the following two parametric equations:

$$\frac{(x-h)^2}{a^2} = cos^2(t)$$
$$\frac{(y-k)^2}{b^2} = sin^2(t)$$

Taking the square root of both sides of each equation we get:

$$\frac{x-h}{a} = cos(t)$$
$$\frac{y-k}{b} = sin(t)$$

Then we multiply the $x$ equation by $a$, and we multiply the $y$ equation by $b$.

$$x - h = acos(t)$$
$$y - k = bsin(t)$$

Then we add each equation's constant to both sides, resulting in the following equations:

$$x(t) = acos(t) + h$$
$$y(t) = bsin(t) + k$$

These are the parametric equations for both the $x$ and $y$ for an ellipse. Now that we've parameterized the general equation for an ellipse let's do the same for the general equation for hyperbolas. Unlike circles and ellipses hyperbolas have two different general formulas:

$$\frac{(x-h)^2}{a^2} - \frac{(y-k)^2}{b^2} = 1$$

$$\frac{(y-k)^2}{b^2} - \frac{(x-h)^2}{a^2} = 1$$

Just like for circles and ellipses the first step is the same for hyperbolas, the equations to one of the Pythagorean identities. However, unlike for circles and ellipses we will be using the Pythagorean identity,

$$sec^2(t) = 1 + tan^2(t)$$

If we rearrange this identity we get,

$$sec^2(t) - tan^2(t) = 1$$

Using this form of the identity we can begin equating parts of the identity and general equation of the hyperbola to each other. Let's begin with the first equation for the hyperbola:

$$\frac{(x-h)^2}{a^2} - \frac{(y-k)^2}{b^2} = 1$$

The first step to find the parametric equations for $x$ and $y$, shown below:

$$sec^2(t) = \frac{(x-h)^2}{a^2}$$

$$tan^2(t) = \frac{(y-k)^2}{b^2}$$

Next, take the square root of both sides of each equation.

$$\frac{x-h}{a} = sec(t)$$
$$\frac{y-k}{b} = tan(t)$$

Then, multiply both sides of each equation by the constants in the denominator.

$$x - h = asec(t)$$
$$y - k = btan(t)$$

After that, add the constants to both sides of each equation.

$$x(t) = asec(t) + h$$
$$y(t) = btan(t) + k$$

Now let's do the same as the other general equation for a hyperbola:

$$\frac{(y-k)^2}{b^2} - \frac{(x-h)^2}{a^2} = 1$$

Just like for the first equation we use the Pythagorean identity

$$sec^2(t) - tan^2(t) = 1$$

From here we incorporate $x$ and $y$.

$$\frac{(y-k)^2}{b^2} = sec^2(t)$$
$$\frac{(x-h)^2}{a^2} = tan^2(t)$$

Then, we take the square root of both sides of the equation.

$$\frac{y-k}{b} = sec(t)$$
$$\frac{x-h}{a} = tan(t)$$

Rearranging both sides of each equation yields the following:

$$x(t) = atan(t) + h$$
$$y(t) = bsec(t) + k$$

## Practice Problems

*All 3 of the following questions are to be done without the use of a graphing calculator.*

Questions 1 and 2 will refer to the implicit function below.

$$y^2x^3 - y^2 = 6e^x$$

1. Which of the following correctly solves for y as a positive function of x?

    A. $y = \frac{6e^x}{x^3-1}$

    B. $y = \frac{6e^x}{x^3}$

    C. $y = \sqrt{\frac{6e^x}{x^3-1}}$

    D. $y = \sqrt{\frac{6e^x}{x^3}}$

2. Which of the following is the domain of this implicit equation?

   A. $[1, \infty)$

   B. $(-\infty, \infty)$

   C. $[0, \infty)$

   D. $(1, \infty)$

3. Which of the following is the contains the correct parametric equations for the hyperbola: $\frac{(y-10)^2}{16} - \frac{(x-7)^2}{9} = 1$

   A. $x(t) = 4\sec(t) + 10; \, y(t) = 3\tan(t) + 7$

   B. $x(t) = 4\tan(t) + 10; \, y(t) = 3\sec(t) + 7$

   C. $x(t) = 4\sin(t) + 10; \, y(t) = 3\cos(t) + 7$

   D. $x(t) = 16\sec(t) + 10; \, y(t) = 9\tan(t) + 7$

## Solutions

1. The first step to solve this question is to factor out $y^2$ on the left side of the equation. This gets us $y^2(x^3 - 1) = 6e^x$. The next step is to divide both sides by $(x^3 - 1)$, which gets us $y^2 = \frac{6e^x}{x^3-1}$, this allows us to eliminate choice B and choice D, because these answer choices did not include the $-1$ inside the denominators. After this we must take the square root of both sides. This gets us $y = \pm\sqrt{\frac{6e^x}{x^3-1}}$. The question only asks us to find $y$ as a positive function of $x$, which leaves us with $y = \sqrt{\frac{6e^x}{x^3-1}}$, this also allows to eliminate choice A as it does not include the radical, leaving us with the correct answer: C.

2. The first step in this problem is to get $y$ in terms of $x$, like we did in question 1. This gets us $y = \pm\sqrt{\frac{6e^x}{x^3-1}}$. First thing to note when figuring out the domain is that we can ignore the $\pm$ in the front of the equation, as this only means that there will be two sections of this equation, on above the $x$-axis and one below the $x$-axis. The next thing to note is that there is a radical with an even index, which means that the argument inside the radical, $\frac{6e^x}{x^3-1}$, cannot be negative. Looking at this function we can see that numerator is positive for all values of $x$. The denominator however is not positive for all values of $x$. To solve for the intervals where the denominator is greater than or equal to zero, you must solve the inequality: $x^3 - 1 \geq 0$. The first step in this process is to factor out the polynomial which gets us $(x - 1)(x^2 + x + 1)$. From here we find that the real zeroes are $x = \{1\}$. Now we can test values above and below 1 to see where the

84

function is positive and negative. The best way to do this is to plug in test points into the function $x^3 - 1$. Some good test points would be zero, to test the values below one, and two to test values above one. Plugging in these test points we find that $x^3 - 1$ is positive for all values $x \geq 1$. This allows to eliminate choices B and C, as B extends the domain all the way to $-\infty$ and C included zero within the domain. However, we are not done with this question yet, because the argument inside the radical has a function inside the denominator. The denominator cannot equal 0, as that would be undefined, and thus the $x$-value 1 cannot be included in the solution interval. Thus, the correct answer is D.

3. The first step to solving this problem is to find out what $a, b, h,$ and $k$ are equal to. From looking at the equation of the hyperbola, $\frac{(y-10)^2}{16} - \frac{(x-7)^2}{9} = 1$, we can see that $b^2 = 16$ and $a^2 = 9$. Taking the square root on both sides of these equations we find that $a = 3$ and $b = 4$. Comparing the equation of the hyperbola we have to the general equation for a hyperbola that opens up and down, we can see that $h = 7$ and $k = 10$. From here we can substitute the values into the general parametric equations of a hyperbola of this form: $x(t) = a\tan(t) + h$ and $y(t) = b\sec(t) + k$. Substituting the values for $a, b, h,$ and $k$ in, we get $x(t) = 4\sec(t) + 10$ and $y(t) = 3\tan(t) + 7$, which is answer choice A.

# Module 16: Conic Sections

The next topic is conic sections. These are essentially graphs or figures that are derived from a double cone, shown below. The three sections are parabolas, hyperbolas, ellipses, with circles being a special type of ellipse. There are also three degenerate conics: a point, a line, and intersecting lines. All three of these conic sections pass through the vertex of the double cone.

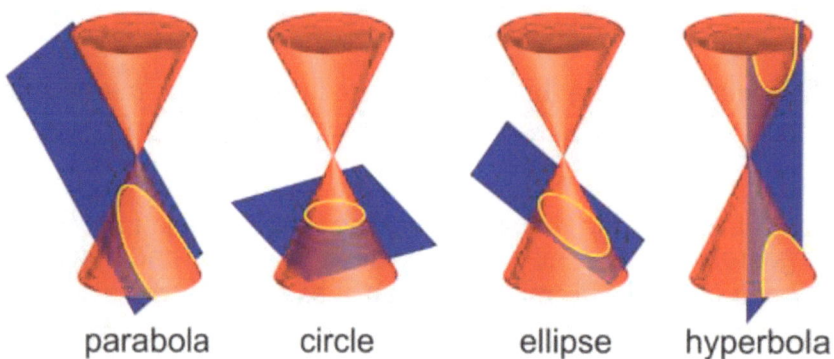

Figure 41 (5). This image was taken from ck12.org. In each of the double cones, the angle, and places that the plane intersects the double cone impacts the conic section formed. Notice how the circle is a type of ellipse in which the entire plane is the same vertical distance down from the vertex. Also, through this image, one can visualize the degenerate conics, as the point is the vertex, line would glide the edges of each cone and pass through the center, the same happening twice for intersecting lines.

To discuss all these functions, we'll use vertex form. First, parabolas. Parabolas that open to the left or to the right, and thus aren't functions, are in the form: $x - h = a(y - k)^2$. Parabolas that open up or down, as you might already know, are in the form: $y - k = a(x - h)^2$, In both of these forms, the vertex is the point $(h, k)$ and the $a$ value is not zero.

Although most might already know that a parabola is the graph of a quadratic, there's another definition for parabolas that also explains their shape. Similar to how a circle is the set of all points that are an equal distance (the radius) from a given point (center), a parabola is the set of all points that are equal distance to a line and a point. In other words, for any given point on the parabola, it is an equal distance away from a certain line and point. This line is known as the directrix, while the point is known as the focus. The directrix is perpendicular to the axis of symmetry and does not intersect the parabola, while the focus, though not being a part of the parabola either, can be thought of as inside the parabola. The focus lies on the axis of symmetry and using the distance from the focus to the vertex, we can keep going in that direction to get a point on the directrix, and thus the line. This specific distance is called $p$, and it is equal to $\frac{1}{|4a|}$, the same $a$ as the coefficient of the vertex form. The line parallel to the directrix that connects the focus to the parabola is known as the latus rectum, and its length is equal to $\frac{1}{|a|}$.

Figure 42 (1). This graph was made on Desmos.com. The red parabola is the graph of $y = \frac{1}{4}x^2$. The purple and black line segments both represent $p$, with a length of 1 in this case. The blue line represents the directrix, with an equation of $y = -1$. The green point represents the focus, with coordinates $(0, 1)$. Finally, the orange line segment represents the latus rectum, with a length of 4.

With the knowledge of these concepts, it's now must easier to derive the equation of a parabola. Suppose a parabola with vertex $(-3, 7)$ and focus $(-3, 5)$. What is the equation for this graph? For starters, the $h$ and $k$ values are $-3$ and $-7$, respectively. Furthermore, the $p$ value must be $-2$, as the focus is 2 units under the vertex. To find the $a$ value, use the equation $p = \frac{1}{4a}$, yielding that $a$ is $-\frac{1}{8}$. Thus, the equation for the parabola is $y = -\frac{1}{8}(x + 3)^2 + 7$.

Let's attempt another problem. Given focus $(4, 12)$ and directrix $x = -6$, what is the equation of the parabola? In this case, the directrix is a vertical line, indicating that the parabola faces sideways. Because the vertex must be in the middle of the focus and directrix, its coordinates are $(-1, 12)$. Using the vertex and focus, the $p$ value is found to be 5. Using the equation $p = \frac{1}{4a}$, $a$ is found to be $\frac{1}{20}$. Thus, the equation for the parabola is $x = \frac{1}{20}(y - 12)^2 - 1$.

Next are hyperbolas, which appear to be like two parabolas facing opposite directions. Just like parabolas, there are two general forms. If the hyperbola opens to the left and right, it has the form $\frac{(x-h)^2}{a^2} - \frac{(y-k)^2}{b^2} = 1$. If it opens and down, it has the form $\frac{(y-k)^2}{a^2} - \frac{(x-h)^2}{b^2} = 1$.

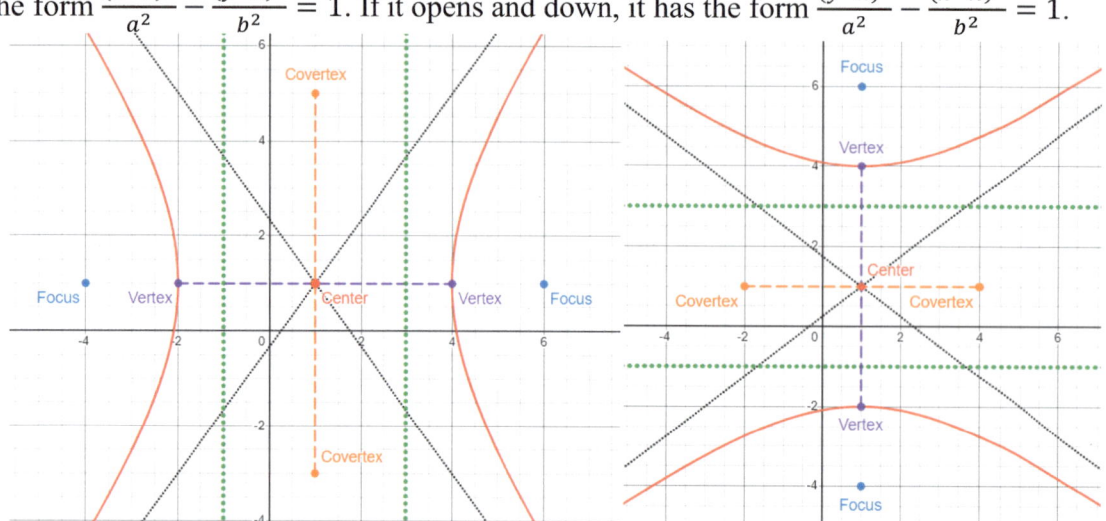

Figures 43 (1) and 44 (1). The graphs above were made on Desmos.com. The graph on the left is of the equation $\frac{(x-1)^2}{9} - \frac{(y-1)^2}{16} = 1$, while the graph on the right is of the equation $\frac{(y-1)^2}{9} - \frac{(x-1)^2}{16} = 1$. The vertices, covertices, foci, and center of each graph are labeled. The dotted green vertical lines on the function on the left are the directrices, with equations $x = -1$ and $x = 3$, while the dotted green horizontal lines on the function on the right are directrices with the equations $y = -1$ and $y = 3$. The dashed purple lines in both graphs that connect the vertices are the transverse axes, while the dashed lines that connect the covertices are the conjugate axes. The slant asymptotes of the function on the left have the equation $y - 1 = \pm\frac{4}{3}(x - 1)$ while the slant asymptotes of the function on the right have the equation $y - 1 = \pm\frac{3}{4}(x - 1)$.

Notice, the one that mainly opens in the $x$ axis has the $x$ on the left in the equation, while the one that mainly opens in the $y$ axis has the $y$ on the left in the equation. The $a$ and $b$ values represent half of the length of the transverse and conjugate axes, respectively. The transverse axis is the axis that connects the vertices. The endpoints of the conjugate axis are known as covertices. The slant asymptotes of the hyperbola pass through the corners of the rectangle made from the conjugate axis and the transverse axis. $(h, k)$ are the coordinates of the center, which doesn't lie on either part of the hyperbola, but rather is in between. Each section of the hyperbola has a vertex, and the coordinates of these are found by $(h \pm a, k)$ or $(h, k \pm a)$, with the former being for left-right opening hyperbolas and the latter being for up-down opening hyperbolas. Along with that, each section of the hyperbola has a focus, found by the coordinates $(h \pm c, k)$ or $(h, k \pm c)$, where $c = \sqrt{a^2 + b^2}$. The directrices of hyperbolas are found at $(h \pm (c - a), k)$ or $(h, k \pm (c - a))$. The slant asymptotes are in the form $(y - k) = \pm\frac{b}{a}(x - h)$.

Now, if you're told that you have a hyperbola with vertices $(2, 4)$ and $(6, 4)$, with conjugate axis length 8, what is the equation of the hyperbola? Well based off this information, we know that the center is at $(4, 4)$, as the center is in the middle of the vertices. Furthermore, we know the length of the transverse axis is 4, as it is the axis that connects the vertices. Thus, our $a$-value is 2. We also know our $b$-value is 4, because the conjugate axis has length 8. Now that we have all the information together, we can set up the equation $\frac{(x-4)^2}{4} - \frac{(y-4)^2}{16} = 1$.

Let's do another one. Given one vertex $(0, 9)$ and covertices $(-4, 6)$ and $(4, 6)$, what is the equation of the hyperbola and where are the foci located? From this information, we know that the center of the parabola is $(0, 6)$, and thus the $b$-value must be 4. Furthermore, because the vertex is 3 units away from the center, the $a$-value is 3. From this information, we find that the equation of the hyperbola is $\frac{(y-6)^2}{9} - \frac{x^2}{16} = 1$. To find the foci, we must find $c$. To do this, we use the equation $c = \sqrt{a^2 + b^2}$, yielding $c = 5$. Finally, foci are located at distance c away from the center. Thus, the foci are located at the points $(0, 11)$ and $(0, 1)$.

The final conic section is the ellipse. These are in the form $\frac{(x-h)^2}{a^2} + \frac{(y-k)^2}{b^2} = 1$ or $\frac{(x-h)^2}{b^2} + \frac{(y-k)^2}{a^2} = 1$. In the case of ellipses, $a$ is larger than $b$, where $a$ and $b$ both are radii of the ellipse, and whether they are vertical or horizontal radii depend on if they are under $y$ or $x$, respectively.

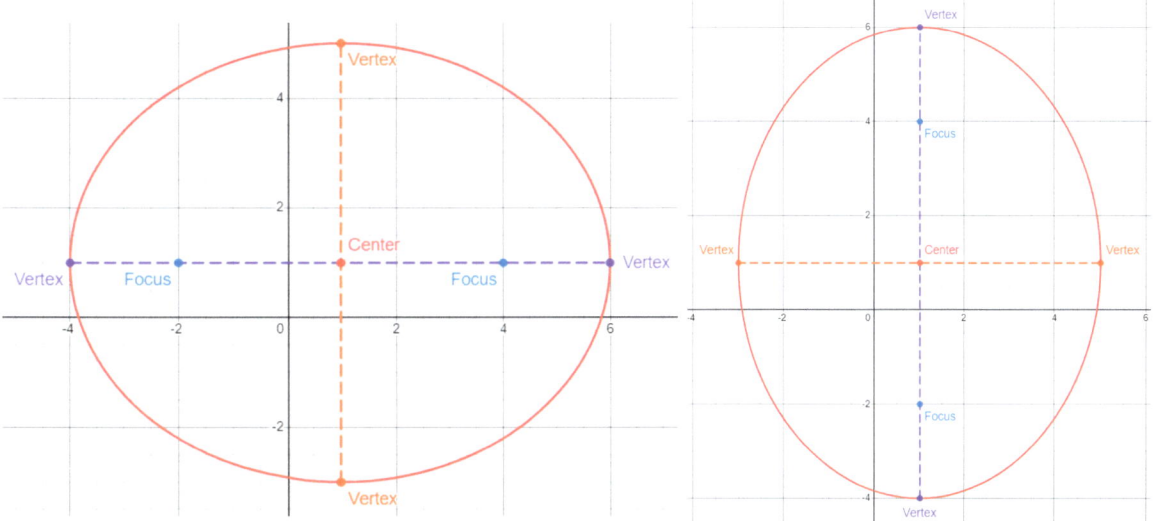

Figures 45 (1) and 46 (1). The graphs above were made on Desmos.com. The graph on the left is of the equation $\frac{(x-1)^2}{25} + \frac{(y-1)^2}{16} = 1$, while the graph on the right is of the function $\frac{(x-1)^2}{16} + \frac{(y-1)^2}{25} = 1$. The center, foci, and vertices are labeled. For the graph on the left, the horizontal dashed line connecting the vertices is the major axis while the vertical dashed line connecting the other two vertices is the minor axis. For the graph on the right, the vertical dashed line connecting the vertices is the major axis while the horizontal dashed line connecting the other two vertices is the minor axis.

The radii do not have the same value all throughout the ellipse, as displayed by the horizontal radius length versus the vertical radius length, unless $a = b$. In that case, a circle, a special type of ellipse, would be present. Once again, the center is located at $(h, k)$. The vertices are in the form $(h \pm a, k)$ and $(h, k \pm b)$ if $a$ is under $x$, and $(h \pm b, k)$ and $(h, k \pm a)$ if $a$ is under $y$. Thus, there are no covertices. The axes connect the vertices, where the longer axis is called the major axis while the shorter axis is called the minor axis. Foci lie on the major axis and are found at $(h \pm c, k)$ or $(h, k \pm c)$, where $c = \sqrt{a^2 - b^2}$. The eccentricity of the ellipse is found by the equation $e = \frac{c}{a}$. The eccentricity is a value used to define the shape of the graph, and the closer it gets to 0, the more the graph looks like a circle, while the closer it gets to 1, the more it looks like two straight lines. Another definition for a circle, therefore, is an ellipse with an eccentricity of 0.

Suppose an ellipse with the equation $\frac{x^2}{144} + \frac{(y+5)^2}{169} = 1$. What are the coordinates for all four of the vertices? From the equation, it's clear that the vertex lies at the point $(0, -5)$, and the $a$-value is 13 while the $b$-value is 12. To find the coordinates of the vertices, first add and subtract 12 from the $x$-values for 2 of the vertices, then add and subtract 13 from the $y$-values for the other 2 vertices. Thus, the coordinates of the vertices are $(-12, -5)$, $(12, -5)$, $(0, -18)$, $(0, 8)$.

For a more challenging problem, suppose an ellipse with vertices $(4, 8)$, $(6, 12)$, and $(6, f)$, where $f$ is an integer. What is the equation for this ellipse and what is the value of $f$? Based on the coordinates of the first two vertices, it's clear that they lie on different axes. The third vertex has an $x$-value of 6, and therefore a vertical axis is at $x = 6$. Because the first point, $(4, 8)$, is equidistant from this vertical axis with another point, the other point must have the coordinates $(8, 8)$. Furthermore, because both points share a $y$-value of 8, the horizontal axis exists at $y = 8$, and combining this with the location of the vertical axis, the coordinates of the center are $(6, 8)$. Also, using these points, its clear that the value of $f$ must be 4, as it must be equidistant from the horizontal axis with the point $(6, 12)$. Using these values, the length of the vertical axis is 8 while the length of the horizontal axis is 4, and thus the vertical axis is the major axis and the $a$-value is 4, while the horizontal axis is the minor axis and the $b$-value is 2. Piecing all this information together, the equation of the ellipse is $\frac{(x-6)^2}{4} + \frac{(y-8)^2}{16} = 1$.

## Practice Problems

*A graphing calculator is permitted for all three of the following questions*

1. Find the zeros of the parabola with focus $\left(\frac{1}{2}, -\frac{21}{8}\right)$ and LR of length 2, given that the parabola faces up.

    a. $\left(\frac{1}{2}, 0\right)$ and $\left(-\frac{25}{8}, 0\right)$

    b. $\left(\frac{1}{2}, 0\right)$ and $\left(-\frac{21}{8}, 0\right)$

    c. $(-1, 0)$ and $\left(\frac{3}{2}, 0\right)$

    d. $(-2, 0)$ and $(3, 0)$

2. Given a hyperbola with center $(4, 5)$, vertex $(4, 8)$, and conjugate axis of length 8, find the $y$-values for the points with a $x$-value of 8.

    a. $y = \pm 4$

    b. $y = 5 \pm \frac{4\sqrt{7}}{3}$

c. $y = 2, y = 8$

d. $y = \frac{1}{4}, \frac{31}{4}$

3. Given an ellipse with minor axis endpoint $(3, 12)$ and horizontal major axis length of 18 at $y = 4$, which of the following gives the equation of the graph when reflected across the x-axis?

a. $\frac{(x-3)^2}{81} + \frac{(y+4)^2}{64} = 1$

b. $\frac{(x-3)^2}{81} + \frac{(y-4)^2}{64} = 1$

c. $\frac{(x-3)^2}{18} + \frac{(-y-4)^2}{64} = 1$

d. $\frac{(-x-3)^2}{81} + \frac{(y-4)^2}{64} = 1$

## Solutions

1. In this question, the zeros of the parabola must be found. To do so, the equation of the parabola must be found first. Using the length of the LR, the $a$ value is found to be $\frac{1}{2}$. From this, the $p$-value is found to be 2, and thus the vertex is $\left(\frac{1}{2}, -\frac{25}{8}\right)$. Now we can create the vertex form equation of the parabola, which is $y = \frac{1}{2}\left(x - \frac{1}{2}\right)^2 - \frac{25}{8}$. From here, because a graphing calculator is allowed, this can be directly input into the calculator to find the roots. However, if you intend to do this question by hand, then expand out the parabola to get $y = \frac{1}{2}x^2 - \frac{1}{2}x - \frac{24}{8}$ and factor out the $\frac{1}{2}$ to get $y = x^2 - x - 6$, and using more factoring the zeros are found to be $(-2, 0)$ and $(3, 0)$. Thus, answer choice D is the correct option.

2. In this question, the y values for a given x value on the hyperbola must be found. To do this, the equation of the hyperbola must be found. Using a vertex of 8, the a-value must be 3. The b-value must be 4, based on the conjugate axis length. Combining this with the center of $(4, 5)$, the equation of the hyperbola is $\frac{(y-4)^2}{9} - \frac{(x-5)^2}{16} = 1$. To find the y values for an x-value of 8, substitute it into the equation and solve for y, yielding $y = 4 \pm \frac{15}{4}$, but because these are numbers that can be combined, it is rewritten as $y = \frac{1}{4}, \frac{31}{4}$, and thus option D is the correct answer choice.

3. In this question, the equation of the vertical reflection of the ellipse must be found. To do this, the equation of the ellipse from the given points must be found, and then $-y$ should be substituted in for y. Given that one of the vertices is $(3, 12)$ and the horizontal major axis is at $y = 4$, the center of the ellipse is $(3, 4)$, and thus the b-

value is 8. Furthermore, because the length of the major axis is 18, the a-value is 9. Using this information, the equation of the ellipse is $\frac{(x-3)^2}{81} + \frac{(y-4)^2}{64} = 1$. To find the vertical reflection, substitute $-y$ for $y$, yielding the equation $\frac{(x-3)^2}{81} + \frac{(-y-4)^2}{64} = 1$. However, notice that a $-1$ can be factored from the y expression, and because it is being squared, it converts to 1. Thus, another way to represent the equation for the ellipse is $\frac{(x-3)^2}{81} + \frac{(y+4)^2}{64} = 1$. Therefore, option A is the correct answer choice.

# Module 17: Vectors and Vector-Valued Functions

So far, all the quantities we have discussed are scalars, quantities that have magnitude but lack direction. However, there is another type of quantity called a vector, a quantity that has both magnitude and direction. Vectors are defined by line segments with both a magnitude and direction. Vectors are denoted by a letter with an arrow above it, for example $\vec{v}$. The magnitude of a vector is determined by the length of the vector and the direction of a vector is determined by the angle it makes with the positive $x$-axis. Vectors are defined by their components in the form of $\langle a, \ b \rangle$. Oftentimes vectors you will be given two points on a vector, one at the tail, $(x_1, y_1)$ and one at the tip, $(x_2, y_2)$. To find the component form of such vectors all you would need to do is to subtract the $x$-component of the tail from the $x$-component of the tip, and the $y$-component of the tail from the $y$-component of the tip, $\langle x_2 - x_1, \ y_2 - y_1 \rangle$.

The magnitude of a vector is a scalar quantity, which is found by taking the square root of the sum of the squares of the $x$ and $y$ components.

$$\|\vec{v}\| = \sqrt{x^2 + y^2}$$

Looking at this formula we can tell that this formula is exactly like the Pythagorean theorem. In fact, vectors can be thought of as the hypotenuse of the triangle formed by the $x$ and $y$ components of said vector. Using this idea, we can use right triangle trigonometry to define a vector's components in terms of its magnitude.

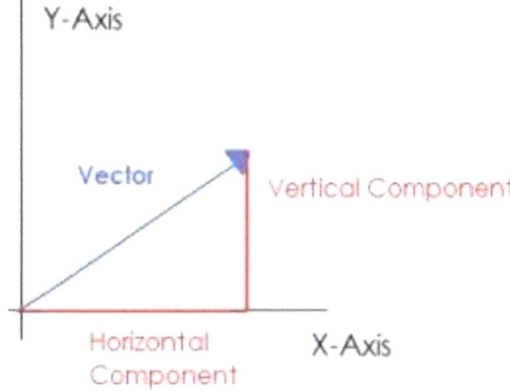

Figure 47 (6). This image was taken from jakeweston.com. The image shows a vector in the cartesian coordinate plane along with its components. The $x$-component lies on the $x$-axis and goes form the tail of the vector at the origin to the $x$-coordinate of the tip of the vector. The $y$-component starts on the $x$-axis where the $x$-coordinate of the tip of the vector is and extends up to the tip of the vector. The arrangement of the vector with its components creates a right triangle.

Let's take the vector $\vec{v}$, with magnitude $\|\vec{v}\|$ and forms an angle $\theta$ with the positive x-axis. The components $\vec{v}$ of would be $\langle \|\vec{v}\| \cos(\theta), \ \|\vec{v}\| \sin(\theta) \rangle$.

Now let's talk about addition, subtraction, and scalar multiplication of vectors. First let's discuss scalar multiplication. For this let's use the vector $\vec{a} = \langle 7, \ 8 \rangle$. Let's then multiply this vector by 2 getting us $2\vec{a}$. $2\vec{a} = \langle 2(7), \ 2(8) \rangle = \langle 14, \ 16 \rangle$. From this we can see that all scalar multiplication is just multiplying the scalar quantity to each component of the vector.

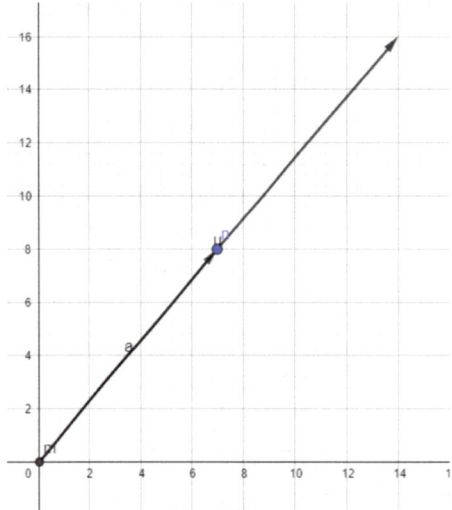

Figure 48 (7). This image was created on GeoGebra. The first vector on the graph represents vector $\vec{a}$ and the second vector $\vec{u}$ represents $2\vec{a}$.

Next let's discuss the addition of two vectors. Imagine two vectors $\vec{m} = \langle 4,\ 2 \rangle$ and $\vec{n} = \langle 7,\ 5 \rangle$. To add these vectors, add up their respective components, so $\vec{m} + \vec{n} = \langle 4 + 7,\ 2 + 5 \rangle = \langle 11,\ 7 \rangle$. Graphically the addition of two vectors can be represented by placing the first vector with its tail at the origin and placing the second vector on the head of the first vector. The vector that is created placing its tail at the tail of the first vector and head at the head of the second vector is the resultant vector, or the sum of the first two vectors.

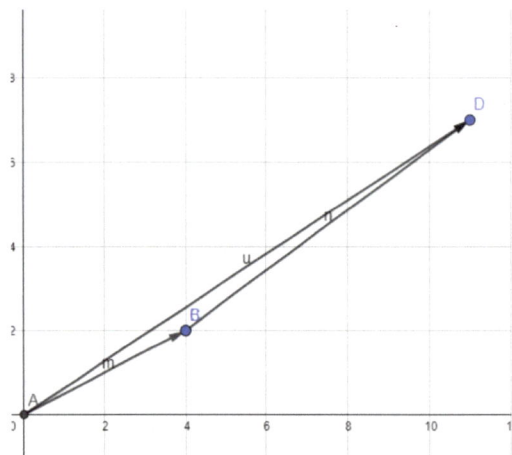

Figure 49 (7). This image was created on GeoGebra. The first vector on the graph represents $\vec{m}$ and the second vector represents $\vec{n}$. The third vector $\vec{u}$ represents $\vec{m} + \vec{n}$.

Now let's discuss the subtraction of two vectors. Let's use the same vectors $\vec{m}$ and $\vec{n}$ for this example. The resultant of the subtraction of these two vectors is $\vec{m} - \vec{n}$, which could just be thought of as $\vec{m} + (-\vec{n})$ We know that $\vec{m} = \langle 4, 2 \rangle$ and $\vec{n} = \langle 7,\ 5 \rangle$, and using scalar multiplication we can determine that $-\vec{n} = \langle -7,\ -5 \rangle$. Adding these two vectors we get $\vec{m} + (-\vec{n}) = \vec{m} - \vec{n} = \langle 4 + (-7),\ 2 + (-5) \rangle = \langle -3,\ -3 \rangle$. Graphically this would be represented the same way as the addition of two vectors, but instead of adding the two vectors as so you graph the first vector normally, then you add the negative version of the second vector to the tip of the first vector and draw the new resultant vector from the tail of the first vector the tip of the second.

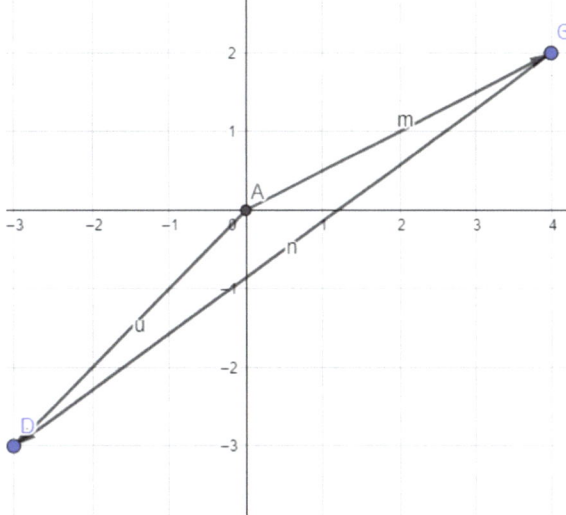

Figure 50 (7). This image was created on GeoGebra. The first vector on the graph represents $\vec{m}$ and the second vector represents $\vec{n}$. The third vector $\vec{u}$ represents $\vec{m} - \vec{n}$.

    Next, the dot product of two vectors. Imagine two vectors $\vec{a} = \langle 2, \ 3 \rangle$ and $\vec{b} = \langle 1, \ 5 \rangle$. The dot product of these two vectors would be represented by $\vec{a} \cdot \vec{b}$. To find the dot product, find the sum of the products of the $x$ and $y$ components, which would mean $\vec{a} \cdot \vec{b} = 2(1) + 5(3) = 2 + 15 = 17$. From this example we can determine that the algebraic definition of a dot product for two vectors $\vec{m} = \langle m_x, m_y \rangle$ and $\vec{n} = \langle n_x, n_y \rangle$ is $\vec{m} \cdot \vec{n} = m_x n_x + m_y n_y$. Let's say we have two vectors $\vec{v}$ and $\vec{w}$ such that the magnitude of each vector is $\|\vec{v}\| = 8$, and $\|\vec{w}\| = 2$, and the angle between the two vectors is $\theta = \frac{\pi}{3}$. The dot product would be equal to $\|\vec{v}\| \|\vec{w}\| \cos \frac{\pi}{3} = 8(2) \left( \frac{1}{2} \right) = 8$. Using this example, we can that the geometric definition of a dot product for two vectors $\vec{u}$ and $\vec{v}$ is $\vec{u} \cdot \vec{v} = \|\vec{u}\| \|\vec{v}\| \cos \theta$, where $\|\vec{u}\| \|\vec{v}\|$ is the magnitude of the two vectors and $\theta$ is the angle between the two vectors. Rearranging this formula for the dot product we can determine that the angle between two vectors is $\theta = \cos^{-1} \left( \frac{\vec{u} \cdot \vec{v}}{\|\vec{u}\| \|\vec{v}\|} \right)$. If the dot product of two vectors is zero the two vectors are considered orthogonal, and this happens when two vectors are perpendicular to each other. From these two examples we can tell that the dot product produces a scalar quantity, not a new vector, which begs the question, what does a dot product represent? The best way to think of a dot product is as a rating of how well the first vector maps the second vector, or how closely the first vector and second vector point in the same direction.

    The next topic we will discuss is unit vectors. Unit vectors are vectors with a magnitude of 1. We can turn any vector into a unit vector by dividing by components and magnitude of the vector by the reciprocal of the magnitude of the vector. Let's take vector $\vec{b} = \langle 6, \ 8 \rangle$ as an example. Firstly, $\|\vec{b}\| = 10$, so to turn $\vec{b}$ into a unit vector you must multiply the components and the magnitude of the vector by $\frac{1}{10}$. This would get us $\frac{1}{10} \vec{b} = \langle \frac{3}{5}, \ \frac{4}{5} \rangle$, and this vector would have a magnitude of 1. The purpose of unit vectors is to represent vectors in linear combination form. This is where vectors are represented by scaled unit vectors $\hat{\imath}$, a unit vector parallel to the x-axis, and $\hat{j}$, a unit vector parallel to the y-axis. Represented in component form, $\hat{i} = \langle 1,\ 0 \rangle$ and $\hat{j} = \langle 0,\ 1 \rangle$. Let's take vector $\vec{c} = \langle 7,\ 3 \rangle$ and represent it in linear combination form. In linear combination form vector $\vec{c} = 7\hat{i} + 3\hat{j}$. This is because we can think of the components of vector c as scalar being multiplied to the unit vectors $\hat{i}$ and $\hat{j}$. By doing this we get $\vec{c} = \langle 7(1), 7(0) \rangle + \langle 3(0), 3(1) \rangle = \langle 7,\ 0 \rangle + \langle 0,\ 3 \rangle = \langle 7,\ 3 \rangle$, getting us back to the component from. Using this property, we can say that vector $\vec{v} = \langle a,\ b \rangle$ in linear combination form would be $\vec{v} = a\hat{i} + b\hat{j}$. Now let's discuss our final topic for this section, vector-valued functions. Previously we learned about parametric equations, where x and y were both defined by a variable $t$ to where $f(t) = (x(t), y(t))$. Now what if instead of considering $f(t)$ as a parametrically defined function, we thought of it as a vector valued function. This changes the function to where, instead of the outputs being points, the outputs are vectors. These vectors are formed with their tail at the origin and their tips as the outputs of the function, and the function is graphed by connecting all the tips of the vectors. Vector valued functions are mainly used to model real world concepts, such as position or velocity. The best way to show this is through examples. Let's take the vector-valued function $\vec{v}(t) = \langle t^2 - 3,\ t + 4 \rangle$ to represent the velocity of a particle as a function of time t as it moves in the cartesian coordinate system. Is this function moving in the positive or negative y-direction at $t = 2$? To figure this out we can first plug in $t = 2$ into our vector-values function getting us $\vec{v}(2) = \langle (2)^2 - 3, 2 + 4 \rangle = \langle 4 - 3, 6 \rangle = \langle 1, 6 \rangle$. At $t = 2, \vec{v}(t)$ produces the vector $\langle 1, 6 \rangle$, and to figure out in which direction the function is moving on the y-axis, we must look at the y-component of the vector, which usually represents motion in the vertical direction. If the y-component is positive the particle is moving in the positive y-direction and if the y-component is negative the particle is moving in the negative y-direction. The y-component at $t = 2$ is 6, which is positive which means that the particle is moving in the positive y-direction. For this same function, is the particle moving in the positive or negative x-direction at $t = 4$? Just like we did to figure out if the particle is moving in the positive or negative y-direction, we first must plug in t = 4 into our vector valued function, getting us $\vec{v}(4) = \langle (4)^2 - 3, 4 + 4 \rangle = \langle 16 - 3, 8 \rangle = \langle 13, 8 \rangle$. At $t = 4$, the function produces the vector $\langle 13,\ 8 \rangle$, and to figure out whether the particle is moving in the positive or negative x-direction we must look at the horizontal component of the vector. If the horizontal component is positive the particle is moving in the positive x-direction, if the horizontal component is negative the particle is moving negative x-direction. At time $t = 4$ the x-component is 13, which is positive meaning that the particle is moving in the positive x-direction at time t = 4. For this same vector valued function what is the speed of the particle at time $t = 3$. The speed of the particle is a scalar quantity that is represented by the magnitude of the velocity vector at time $t$. The first step to finding the speed is the same as for the previous problems, plug $t = 3$ into the function. This gets us $\vec{v}(3) = \langle (3)^2 - 3, 3 + 4 \rangle = \langle 9 - 3, 7 \rangle = \langle 6, 7 \rangle$. Now that we have the velocity vector at $t = 3$, we can now find the speed, which is just $\|\vec{v}(3)\|$. This gets us $\sqrt{(6)^2 + (7)^2} = \sqrt{36 + 49} = \sqrt{85}$ which is the speed of the particle at time $t = 3$. Something to note when solving problems that involve vector-valued functions is that they might specify that the positive and negative x-directions are east and west respectively and that the positive and negative y-directions are north and south respectively.

## Practice Problems

*All 3 of the following questions are to be done without the use of a graphing calculator.*

1. What is the magnitude of vector $\vec{v} = \langle 24, 10 \rangle$

   a. 27

   b. 34

   c. 26

   d. $\sqrt{586}$

2. Given vector $\vec{a} = \langle 5, 4 \rangle$ and vector $\vec{b} = \langle 7, 2 \rangle$, find $3\vec{a} + 4\vec{b}$ as a sum of the unit vectors $\hat{\imath}$ and $\hat{\jmath}$.

   a. $43\hat{\imath} + 20\hat{\jmath}$

   b. $33\hat{\imath} + 20\hat{\jmath}$

   c. $43\hat{\imath} + 30\hat{\jmath}$

   d. $20\hat{\imath} + 43\hat{\jmath}$

3. The vector-valued function $\vec{v}(t) = \langle x(t), y(t) \rangle$ represents the velocity of a particle moving in the cartesian coordinate system for time $t$. If the speed of the particle at time $t = 4$ is 25 and is moving at an angle of $\theta = \frac{2\pi}{3}$ with respect to the x-axis. What direction is the velocity in both the horizontal and vertical directions?

   a. Positive $x$ direction and negative $y$ direction

   b. Negative $x$ and $y$ direction

   c. Positive $x$ direction and positive $y$ direction

   d. Negative $x$ direction and positive $y$ direction

## Solutions

1. For this question all you must do is plug the components of $\vec{v}$ into the formula for the magnitude,
$$\|\vec{v}\| = \sqrt{x^2 + y^2}$$
Plugging in we get $\sqrt{24^2 + 10^2} = \sqrt{576 + 100} = \sqrt{676} = 26$, which is answer choice c, making it the correct answer.

2. The question is asking you to find $3\vec{a} + 4\vec{b}$ in linear combination form when $\vec{a} = \langle 5, 4 \rangle$ and $\vec{b} = \langle 7, 2 \rangle$. Firstly, we have to find the values of $3\vec{a}$ and $4\vec{b}$. For this all we must do is scalar multiplication, and doing so we get $3\vec{a} = \langle 3(5), 3(4) \rangle = \langle 15, 12 \rangle$ and $4\vec{b} = \langle 4(7), 4(2) \rangle = \langle 28, 8 \rangle$. Converting both vectors to linear combination form we get $3\vec{a} = 15\hat{\imath} + 12\hat{\jmath}$ and $4\vec{b} = 28\hat{\imath} + 8\hat{\jmath}$. Adding up these vectors we get $3\vec{a} + 4\vec{b} = (15 + 28)\hat{\imath} + (12 + 8)\hat{\jmath} = 43\hat{\imath} + 20\hat{\jmath}$, which matches answer choice a, making that the correct answer.

3. In this question we are given a vector valued function that represents the velocity of a particle as it moves throughout the cartesian coordinate plane. We are told that at time $t = 4$ the speed of the particle is 25 and the angle it makes with respect with the positive x-axis is $\theta = \frac{2\pi}{3}$. Firstly, we know that the speed is the magnitude of the velocity vector at $t = 4$, and the angle made with the positive x-axis is $\theta = \frac{2\pi}{3}$. Using this information, we can find the components of the vector. We know that if you have the magnitude of a vector, $\|v\|$ and direction angle $\theta$, the components of the vector will be $\langle \|v\| \cos\theta, \|v\| \sin\theta \rangle$, and if we plug in the speed for the magnitude and $\theta = \frac{2\pi}{3}$ for the direction angle we get $\langle 25 \cos\frac{2\pi}{3}, 25 \sin\frac{2\pi}{3} \rangle$. If we simplify this, we get $\langle 25(-\frac{1}{2}), 25(\frac{\sqrt{3}}{2}) \rangle = \langle -12.5, \frac{25\sqrt{3}}{2} \rangle$. We also know that if the $x$-component is positive the particle is moving in the positive $x$ direction and if the $x$-component is negative the particle is moving in the negative $x$ direction. Similarly, if the $y$-component is negative the particle is moving in the negative $y$ direction and if the $y$-component is positive the particle is moving the positive $y$ direction. The vector that is created when $t = 4$ is $\langle -12.5, \frac{25\sqrt{3}}{2} \rangle$, and from here we can tell that the x-component, $-12.5$, is negative, while the y-component, $\frac{25\sqrt{3}}{2}$, is positive. Therefore, at time $t = 4$ that particle is moving in the negative $x$ direction and positive $y$ direction, which matches answer choice d, making it the correct answer.

# Module 18: Matrices

The final module is about matrices. A matrix is an array of numbers. It's usually classified by its size, in the form of $x$ rows by $y$ columns. Thus, a $3 \times 4$ matrix has 3 rows and 4 columns. Below is an example.

$$A = \begin{bmatrix} 1 & 2 & 3 & 4 \\ 5 & 6 & 7 & 8 \\ 9 & 0 & 1 & 0 \end{bmatrix}$$

Any specific term in the matrix can be denoted by $X_{yz}$ where $X$ is the name of the matrix, $y$ is the row of the term, and $z$ is the column of the term. Thus, $A_{23}$ is 7, as it is in the 2nd row and third column. $A_{14}$, on the other hand, is 4.

To add or subtract matrices, you can directly overlay the matrices and add the term from each spot on the matrix to the corresponding spot on the other matrix. Thus, the sum of $\begin{bmatrix} 6 & 8 \\ 7 & 9 \end{bmatrix}$ and $\begin{bmatrix} 2 & 3 \\ 4 & 5 \end{bmatrix}$ is $\begin{bmatrix} 8 & 11 \\ 11 & 14 \end{bmatrix}$. Furthermore, the difference between those two is $\begin{bmatrix} 4 & 5 \\ 3 & 4 \end{bmatrix}$.

To multiply matrices, the number of columns in the first matrix must be equal to the number of rows in the second matrix. The specific way to multiply is that the number in the $m$th row and $n$th column of the product matrix is the dot product of the $m$th row of the first matrix with the $n$th column of the second matrix. The resulting matrix will have the same number of rows as the first matrix and columns as the second matrix. An example is below.

$$[2 \quad 4 \quad 5] \times \begin{bmatrix} 3 \\ 4 \\ 6 \end{bmatrix}$$

The first matrix is a $1 \times 3$ and the second is a $3 \times 1$, so the number of rows in the first matrix is equal to the number of columns in the second one. The resulting matrix must be a 1x1 matrix. To calculate the dot product, we do 2 times 3 plus 4 times 4 plus 5 times 6, which sums to 52. Thus, the product matrix is [52].

For another example, suppose the following product:

$$\begin{bmatrix} 7 & 1 & 2 \\ 9 & 3 & 4 \end{bmatrix} \times \begin{bmatrix} 8 & 2 \\ 3 & 9 \\ 6 & 5 \end{bmatrix}$$

The first matrix is $2 \times 3$ while the second is $3 \times 2$, and thus the product matrix will be a $2 \times 2$. Calculating the dot products is as follows:

$$\begin{bmatrix} (7 \times 8) + (1 \times 3) + (2 \times 6) & (7 \times 2) + (1 \times 9) + (2 \times 5) \\ (9 \times 8) + (3 \times 3) + (4 \times 6) & (9 \times 2) + (3 \times 9) + (4 \times 5) \end{bmatrix}$$

This simplifies down to $\begin{bmatrix} 71 & 33 \\ 105 & 65 \end{bmatrix}$.

A special type of matrix involved in multiplication is an identity matrix. For square matrices, these consist of 1s on the diagonal from the top left to the bottom right and 0s everywhere else. Thus, the identity matrix of a $2 \times 2$ matrix is $\begin{bmatrix} 1 & 0 \\ 0 & 1 \end{bmatrix}$. Furthermore, multiplying a matrix by its inverse also results in the identity matrix. For these reasons, an identity matrix in matrix multiplication can be thought of as 1 in traditional multiplication.

There is no matrix division. However, multiplying a matrix by the inverse of the other matrix is the closest way of doing so. Note that this method only applies for square matrices, as only those have inverses. Recall that multiplying a matrix by the inverse of itself produces the identity matrix, in the same way that multiplying a number by its reciprocal produces 1. To find the inverse of a 2 × 2 matrix, use the following formula:

$$inv\begin{bmatrix} a & b \\ c & d \end{bmatrix} = \frac{1}{ad - bc}\begin{bmatrix} d & -b \\ -c & a \end{bmatrix}$$

Note that multiplying a matrix by a constant is done by multiplying each individual term by that constant. The fraction $\frac{1}{ad-bc}$ is known as the determinant of the matrix, and is denoted as det $(A)$ for a matrix $A$. Once again, only square matrices have determinants, and thus its impossible to find the determinant and inverse for a non-square matrix. Furthermore, if the determinant of the square matrix is 0, then the matrix is not invertible and is known as a singular matrix.

To demonstrate this inverse and multiplication, suppose the matrix $\begin{bmatrix} 4 & 6 \\ 2 & 4 \end{bmatrix}$. The determinant is 4, and thus the inverse of the matrix is $\begin{bmatrix} 1 & -\frac{3}{2} \\ -\frac{1}{2} & 1 \end{bmatrix}$.

Multiplying the two matrices is as follows:

$$\begin{bmatrix} 4 & 6 \\ 2 & 4 \end{bmatrix} \times \begin{bmatrix} 1 & -\frac{3}{2} \\ -\frac{1}{2} & 1 \end{bmatrix} = \begin{bmatrix} (4 \times 1) + (6 \times -\frac{1}{2}) & (4 \times -\frac{3}{2}) + (6 \times 1) \\ (2 \times 1) + (4 \times -\frac{1}{2}) & (2 \times -\frac{3}{2}) + (4 \times 1) \end{bmatrix} = \begin{bmatrix} 1 & 0 \\ 0 & 1 \end{bmatrix}$$

Thus, multiplying the matrix by its inverse produced the identity matrix. Let's try a practice problem. What is the inverse of the matrix $\begin{bmatrix} 4 & 3 \\ 5 & 2 \end{bmatrix}$?

To find the inverse, all that needs to be done is plug the given matrix into the formula $inv\begin{bmatrix} a & b \\ c & d \end{bmatrix} = \frac{1}{ad-bc}\begin{bmatrix} d & -b \\ -c & a \end{bmatrix}$. The work is done below:

$$inv\begin{bmatrix} a & b \\ c & d \end{bmatrix} = \frac{1}{ad - bc}\begin{bmatrix} d & -b \\ -c & a \end{bmatrix}$$

$$inv\begin{bmatrix} 4 & 3 \\ 5 & 2 \end{bmatrix} = \frac{1}{(4)(2) - (3)(5)}\begin{bmatrix} 2 & -3 \\ -5 & 4 \end{bmatrix}$$

$$inv\begin{bmatrix} 4 & 3 \\ 5 & 2 \end{bmatrix} = -\frac{1}{7}\begin{bmatrix} 2 & -3 \\ -5 & 4 \end{bmatrix}$$

$$inv\begin{bmatrix} 4 & 3 \\ 5 & 2 \end{bmatrix} = \begin{bmatrix} -\frac{2}{7} & \frac{3}{7} \\ \frac{5}{7} & -\frac{4}{7} \end{bmatrix}$$

Thus, the inverse of the matrix $\begin{bmatrix} 4 & 3 \\ 5 & 2 \end{bmatrix}$ is $\begin{bmatrix} -\frac{2}{7} & \frac{3}{7} \\ \frac{5}{7} & -\frac{4}{7} \end{bmatrix}$. Let's do another practice problem. Given

$A \times B = \begin{bmatrix} 1 & 0 \\ 0 & 1 \end{bmatrix}$, find $B$, where $A = \begin{bmatrix} 5 & 6 \\ 6 & 5 \end{bmatrix}$. Once again, this question is asking to find the inverse matrix of $A$, as if two matrices produce the identity matrix when multiplied by each other, then the matrices are inverses of each other. This is similar to the statement $f(g(x)) = x$ implying that $f(x)$ and $g(x)$ are inverse of each other. Once again, use the formula $inv \begin{bmatrix} a & b \\ c & d \end{bmatrix} = \frac{1}{ad-bc} \begin{bmatrix} d & -b \\ -c & a \end{bmatrix}$.

$$ inv \begin{bmatrix} a & b \\ c & d \end{bmatrix} = \frac{1}{ad - bc} \begin{bmatrix} d & -b \\ -c & a \end{bmatrix} $$

$$ inv \begin{bmatrix} 5 & 6 \\ 6 & 5 \end{bmatrix} = \frac{1}{(5)(5) - (6)(6)} \begin{bmatrix} 5 & -6 \\ -6 & 5 \end{bmatrix} $$

$$ inv \begin{bmatrix} 5 & 6 \\ 6 & 5 \end{bmatrix} = -\frac{1}{11} \begin{bmatrix} 5 & -6 \\ -6 & 5 \end{bmatrix} $$

$$ inv \begin{bmatrix} 5 & 6 \\ 6 & 5 \end{bmatrix} = \begin{bmatrix} -\frac{5}{11} & \frac{6}{11} \\ \frac{6}{11} & -\frac{5}{11} \end{bmatrix} $$

$$ \text{Thus, matrix } B \text{ is } \begin{bmatrix} -\frac{5}{11} & \frac{6}{11} \\ \frac{6}{11} & -\frac{5}{11} \end{bmatrix}. $$

## Practice Problems

*All 3 of the following questions are to be done without the use of a graphing calculator.*

Questions 1, 2, and 3 refer to the following information.

$$ A = \begin{bmatrix} 7 & 6 \\ 0 & 2 \end{bmatrix} \quad B = \begin{bmatrix} 3 & 3 \\ 4 & -4 \end{bmatrix} \quad C = \begin{bmatrix} 1 & 4 \\ 2 & 5 \\ 3 & 6 \end{bmatrix} \quad D = \begin{bmatrix} 7 & 8 & 9 \\ 7 & 7 & 7 \end{bmatrix} $$

1. Which of the following gives $A - BA$?

   a. $\begin{bmatrix} 21 & 24 \\ 28 & 16 \end{bmatrix}$

   b. $\begin{bmatrix} 45 & -3 \\ 8 & 10 \end{bmatrix}$

   c. $\begin{bmatrix} -14 & -18 \\ -28 & -14 \end{bmatrix}$

d. $\begin{bmatrix} -38 & 9 \\ -8 & -8 \end{bmatrix}$

2. Which of the following gives $DC - AB$

   a. $\begin{bmatrix} 105 & -122 \\ -42 & 50 \end{bmatrix}$

   b. $\begin{bmatrix} 45 & -3 \\ 8 & -8 \end{bmatrix}$

   c. $\begin{bmatrix} 50 & 122 \\ 42 & 105 \end{bmatrix}$

   d. $\begin{bmatrix} 5 & 125 \\ 34 & 113 \end{bmatrix}$

3. Which of the following gives $E$, given that $BE = \begin{bmatrix} 1 & 0 \\ 0 & 1 \end{bmatrix}$?

   a. $-\dfrac{1}{24}$

   b. $\begin{bmatrix} -\dfrac{1}{8} & -\dfrac{1}{8} \\ -\dfrac{1}{6} & \dfrac{1}{6} \end{bmatrix}$

   c. $\begin{bmatrix} \dfrac{1}{8} & \dfrac{1}{8} \\ \dfrac{1}{6} & -\dfrac{1}{6} \end{bmatrix}$

   d. Undefined; $B$ does not have an inverse matrix

## Solutions

1. In this question, the task is to find $A - BA$, and in order to do that, first $BA$ must be found. Using principles of matrix multiplication, $BA = \begin{bmatrix} 21 & 24 \\ 28 & 16 \end{bmatrix}$. Thus, $A - BA$ is $\begin{bmatrix} 7 & 6 \\ 0 & 2 \end{bmatrix} - \begin{bmatrix} 21 & 24 \\ 28 & 16 \end{bmatrix} = \begin{bmatrix} -14 & -18 \\ -28 & -14 \end{bmatrix}$, thus C is the correct answer.

2. In this question, the task is to find $DC - AB$, and in order to do that, first $DC$ and $AB$ must be found. Using the rules of matrix multiplication, $DC = \begin{bmatrix} 50 & 122 \\ 42 & 105 \end{bmatrix}$ and $AB = \begin{bmatrix} 45 & -3 \\ 8 & -8 \end{bmatrix}$, thus $DC - AB = \begin{bmatrix} 5 & 125 \\ 34 & 113 \end{bmatrix}$, thus D is the correct answer.

3. In this question, the task is to find the inverse matrix of $B$, and because $B$ is a 2 by 2 matrix, the formula for the inverse is $\frac{1}{ad-bc}\begin{bmatrix} d & -b \\ -c & a \end{bmatrix}$, where $\begin{bmatrix} a & b \\ c & d \end{bmatrix}$ is the initial matrix. Substituting the according values for $B$, the inverse is $\frac{1}{3(-4)-3(4)}\begin{bmatrix} -4 & -3 \\ -4 & 3 \end{bmatrix}$. However, the determinant, $ad - bc$, is equal to 0, and thus there isn't an inverse matrix, making D the correct option.

# Unit 4 Practice Exam

## Section 1, Part A

### Time — 1 hour

### Number of Questions — 21

A CALCULATOR MAY NOT BE USED ON THIS PART OF THE EXAM.

1. Which of the following is the zeros of a parabola with the value of $p = \frac{1}{8}$, and the vertex at the point $(0, -4)$?

    a. $x = \{-2, 2\}$

    b. $x = \{-4, 4\}$

    c. $x = \{-\sqrt{2}, \sqrt{2}\}$

    d. $x = \{-1, 1\}$

2. Given the vector valued function $\vec{v}(t) = \langle t^2 - 2, 2^t \rangle$, which of the following is the magnitude and direction angle when $t = 2$.

    a. $\|\vec{v}(2)\| = 2\sqrt{5}, \theta = \tan^{-1} 2$

    b. $\|\vec{v}(2)\| = 2\sqrt{2}, \theta = \tan^{-1} \frac{4}{3}$

    c. $\|\vec{v}(2)\| = \sqrt{5}, \theta = \frac{\pi}{4}$

    d. $\|\vec{v}(2)\| = 2, \theta = \tan^{-1} \frac{3}{4}$

3. Which of the following is the domain of the implicitly defined equation $y^2 - y^2 \ln(x - 3) = 1$?

    a. $(-\infty, \infty)$

    b. $[0, 3)$

    c. $[3, 3 + e)$

    d. $(3, 3 + e)$

4. The vector valued function $\vec{v}(t) = \langle x(t), y(t) \rangle$ represents the velocity of a particle as it moves through the cartesian coordinate system. At time $t = 2$ the

magnitude of velocity vector is $\|\vec{v}(2)\| = 9$ and a direction angle of $\theta = \frac{\pi}{6}$. Which of the following represents the direction in which the particle is moving in both the horizontal and vertical directions?

    a. East in the horizontal direction South in the vertical direction

    b. West in the horizontal direction South in the vertical direction

    c. East in the horizontal direction North in the vertical direction

    d. West in the horizontal direction North in the vertical direction

5. Given the parametric equations $x = 5t^3 + 2$ and $y = 7t - t^2$ which of the following defines $y$ as a function of x.

    a. $y = 7\sqrt{\frac{x-2}{5}} - \frac{x-2}{5}$

    b. $y = 7\sqrt[3]{\frac{x-2}{5}} - (\frac{x-2}{5})^{\frac{2}{3}}$

    c. $y = \frac{7x-14}{5} - (\frac{x-2}{5})^2$

    d. $y = 7(\frac{x-2}{5})^3 - (\frac{x-2}{5})^6$

6. What is the lowest y-value on the ellipse $\frac{(x+2)^2}{9} + \frac{(y-1)^2}{4} = 1$?

    a. 1

    b. 3

    c. $-5$

    d. $-1$

7. Given a hyperbola with the center at $(2, 4)$, a covertex at $(2, 9)$, and the length of the transverse axis being 8, which of the following could be the equation for the hyperbola?

    a. $\frac{(y-4)^2}{16} - \frac{(x-2)^2}{25}$

    b. $\frac{(y-2)^2}{16} - \frac{(x-4)^2}{25}$

    c. $\frac{(y-4)^2}{25} - \frac{(x-2)^2}{16}$

    d. $\frac{(y-2)^2}{25} - \frac{(x-4)^2}{16}$

Questions 8 and 9 refer to the following information.

$$A = \begin{bmatrix} 3 & -4 \\ 1 & 2 \\ -7 & 1 \end{bmatrix} \quad B = \begin{bmatrix} 0 & 5 \\ -3 & 2 \\ -2 & 4 \end{bmatrix} \quad C = \begin{bmatrix} 5 & 2 & -1 \\ 0 & X & -4 \end{bmatrix} \quad D = \begin{bmatrix} 24 & -17 \\ 31 & 2 \end{bmatrix}$$

8. Which of the following gives $B - A$?

a. $\begin{bmatrix} 3 & -9 \\ 4 & 0 \\ -5 & -3 \end{bmatrix}$

b. $\begin{bmatrix} 3 & 1 \\ -2 & 4 \\ -9 & 5 \end{bmatrix}$

c. $\begin{bmatrix} -3 & 9 \\ -4 & 0 \\ 5 & 3 \end{bmatrix}$

d. $\begin{bmatrix} -4 & -2 \\ 5 & -1 \\ 3 & -11 \end{bmatrix}$

9. Given that $CA = D$, which of the following gives $X$?

   a. $-1$

   b. $-3$

   c. $2$

   d. **3**

10. Find the area of the rectangle created by the transverse axis and conjugate of the hyperbola $\frac{x^2}{49} - \frac{y^2}{81} = 1$?

   a. 256

   b. 63

   c. 252

   d. **3969**

10. Find slopes of the slant asymptotes of the hyperbola $\frac{(y+4)^2}{4} - \frac{(x-2)^2}{9} = 1$?

   a. $-\frac{2}{3}, \frac{2}{3}$

   b. $-\frac{9}{4}, \frac{9}{4}$

   c. $-\frac{1}{2}, \frac{1}{2}$

   d. $-\frac{3}{2}, \frac{3}{2}$

11. What are the coordinates of the center of the hyperbola $4x^2 - y^2 + 24x + 4y = 28$?

   a. $(-3, -2)$

   b. $(3, -2)$

   c. $(-3, 2)$

SimplyEdu's Premier Prep

d. $(3,2)$

12. Which of the following gives the focus for the parabola $x^2 - 8x - y = -18$?

   a. $(4,\frac{7}{4})$

   b. $(4,\frac{9}{4})$

   c. $(4,2)$

   d. $\left(1,\frac{1}{4}\right)$

13. Given parametric equations $x = 3t + 6$ and $y = -9x^2 - 8$, produce an equation for y in terms of t. Furthermore, on the interval $0 \le t \le 3$, what is the lowest y value?

   a. $-9t^2 - 36t - 332; -332$

   b. $-9t^2 - 36t - 332; -2033$

   c. $-81t^2 - 324t - 332; -332$

   d. $-81t^2 - 324t - 332; -2033$

14. Given parametric equations $x = \frac{1}{24}t + \frac{1}{24}$ and $y = 12t + 1$, find the slope of the line made from these equations. Furthermore, given $x = 2$, find y.

   a. $\frac{1}{2}; -10$

   b. $288; 565$

   c. $2; 13$

   d. $24; 47$

15. Given parametric equations $x = \frac{t^2}{4} - 1$ and $y = \frac{t}{5} + 2$, what is the maximum y value of the function on the interval $-5 \le t \le 5$?

   a. 1

   b. 2

   c. 2.4

   d. 3

16. Rewrite the parametric equations $x = t^2 + 2$ and $y = 2t$ in rectangular form.

   a. $y = \pm 2\sqrt{x - 2}$

   b. $y = \frac{x^2}{4} + 2$

c. $y = \frac{x}{2}$

d. $y = \pm\sqrt{x-2}$

17. Rewrite the parametric equations $x = 3\cos\theta$ and $y = 5\sin\theta$ in rectangular form.

   a. $\frac{x}{3} + \frac{y}{5} = 1$

   b. $\frac{x^2}{25} + \frac{y^2}{9} = 1$

   c. $\frac{x^2}{9} + \frac{y^2}{25} = 1$

   d. $\frac{x}{5} + \frac{y}{3} = 1$

Questions 18 through 21 refer to the following information:

$$A = \begin{bmatrix} 1 & -1 \\ 3 & -2 \end{bmatrix} \quad B = \begin{bmatrix} 0 & 2 \\ -2 & 1 \\ -1 & 0 \end{bmatrix} \quad C = \begin{bmatrix} 3 & -3 & -1 \\ 2 & -2 & 4 \end{bmatrix} \quad D = \begin{bmatrix} Y & 0 \\ X & 1 \end{bmatrix}$$

18. Given that $D$ is the identity matrix, which of the following gives the values of $X$ and $Y$?

   a. $X = 1, Y = 0$

   b. $X = 0, Y = 1$

   c. $X = 0, Y = 0$

   d. $X = 1, Y = 1$

19. Using your answer from the previous question, which of the following matrices represents $DC$?

   a. $\begin{bmatrix} 0 & -1 \\ 0 & 4 \end{bmatrix}$

   b. $\begin{bmatrix} 3 & -3 & -1 \\ 2 & -2 & 4 \end{bmatrix}$

   c. $\begin{bmatrix} 0 & -2 & -1 \\ 2 & 1 & 0 \end{bmatrix}$

   d. $\begin{bmatrix} 1 & -1 & 0 \\ 3 & -2 & 1 \end{bmatrix}$

20. Which of the following matrices represents $A - D$?

   a. $\begin{bmatrix} 1 & -1 \\ 3 & -2 \end{bmatrix}$

   b. $\begin{bmatrix} 2 & -1 \\ 3 & -1 \end{bmatrix}$

c. $\begin{bmatrix} 0 & -1 \\ 3 & -3 \end{bmatrix}$

d. $\begin{bmatrix} 3 & -1 \\ 3 & 0 \end{bmatrix}$

21. Which of the following represents $CB - A$?

a. $\begin{bmatrix} 7 & 3 \\ 0 & 2 \end{bmatrix}$

b. $\begin{bmatrix} 6 & 4 \\ -3 & 4 \end{bmatrix}$

c. $\begin{bmatrix} 8 & 2 \\ 3 & 0 \end{bmatrix}$

d. The solution can't be determined; $BC$ is a $3 \times 3$ matrix while $A$ is a $2 \times 2$ matrix.

# Section 1, Part B

## Time — 30 Minutes

## Number of Questions — 9

### A CALCULATOR IS ALLOWED ON THIS PART OF THE EXAM.

Questions 22 through 24 will refer to the following information.

$$\vec{r}(t) = \langle 7^{\sqrt{t}}, \ln(t) \rangle$$

$$\vec{s}(t) = \langle \sec(t), t^2 - 3t \rangle$$

22. Which of the following is the dot product of the vectors produced when $t = 3$?

a. $-22.793$

b. $-28.286$

c. $-29.386$

d. $-26.089$

23. Which of the following is the angle between the two vectors produced when $t = 4$ in radians?

a. $1.908$

b. $74.310$

c. $1.613$

d. 1.895

24. Which of the following is the angle made with the positive x-axis, for $\vec{r}(t) + \vec{s}(t)$ when $t = 6$ in radians?

a. 9.481

b. 1.185

c. 1.344

d. 0.165

Questions 25 and 26 refer to the following information.

$$f(t) = (e^{t^2 + \sin t}, \tan^{-1}(t^e))$$

25. Which of the following is are coordinates of this parametric function at $t = 2$?

a. $(18.344, 1.42)$

b. $(135.544, 1.42)$

c. $(135.544, 1.436)$

d. $(18.344, 1.436)$

26. Which of the following is the distance from the origin of the parametric function at $t = 1$?

a. 6.495

b. 2.829

c. 2.663

d. 6.354

27. Which of the following represents the domain of the implicitly defined function $y^3 \tan^{-1}(x^2) - y^3 = 7x$

a. $(-1.248, 1.248)$

b. $(1.248, \infty)$

c. $(-\infty, -1.248) \cup (-1.248, 1.248) \cup (1.248, \infty)$

d. $(-\infty, -0.886) \cup (-0.886, 0.886) \cup (0.886, \infty)$

Questions 28 through 30 refer to the following information:

$$\vec{u}(t) = \langle e^t, \cos(t) \rangle$$
$$\vec{v}(t) = \langle \pi^t, \sin(t) \rangle$$

28. Which of the following is the value of the dot product of the two vectors when $t = 2$?

    a. 72.549

    b. 72.927

    c. 8.161

    d. 26.450

29. Which of the following is the angle between the two vectors produced when $t = 3$

    a. 2.750

    b. 1.597

    c. 1.571

    d. 0.0538

30. A new vector valued function $\vec{w}(t)$, which is defined by $\vec{u}(t) + \vec{v}(t)$ models the velocity of a particle as it moves in the cartesian coordinate system. At time $t = 2$ the particle is moving

    a. East in the horizontal direction South in the vertical direction

    b. West in the horizontal direction South in the vertical direction

    c. East in the horizontal direction North in the vertical direction

    d. West in the horizontal direction North in the vertical direction

# Section 2, Part A

## Time — 15 Minutes

## Number of Questions — 1

A CALCULATOR IS ALLOWED ON THIS PART OF THE EXAM.

| $t$(s) | 0 | 1 | 2 | 3 | 4 | 5 |
|---|---|---|---|---|---|---|
| $x(t)$(m/s) | 1 | 4.5 | 17.7 | 73.8 | 313.4 | 1314.0 |
| $y(t)$(m/s) | 0.76 | 2.6 | 8.4 | 27.6 | 91.9 | 307.1 |

1. The table of above shows the measured velocities of a particle traveling through an inclined particle accelerator. The time, $t$, is measured in seconds. $x(t)$ represents the velocity of the particle in the x-direction while $y(t)$ represents the particle's velocity in the y-direction, both of which are measured in meters per second. $\vec{v}(t)$ is a vector-valued function that represents the total velocity of the particle, and $\vec{v}(t) = \langle x(t), y(t) \rangle$. Round your answers to 3 decimal places.

    a) Find an exponential regression equation for both $x(t)$ and $y(t)$.

    b) Using the regression equations found in part a) find the angle between the two vectors produced at $t = 2$ and $t = 3$.

    c) State the direction of the particle's velocity at $t = 7$ in both the horizontal and vertical directions

# Section 2, Part B

## Time — 30 Minutes

## Number of Questions — 2

## A CALCULATOR IS NOT ALLOWED ON THIS PART OF THE EXAM.

1. A Ferris Wheel at a new amusement park has an elliptical shape. A person's position on the wheel can be defined by the parametric functions $x = 3\cos t$ and $y = 5\sin t$, where the $xy$ coordinates $(0, 0)$ mark the center of the wheel, $x$ is the horizontal distance of the person, in meters, $y$ is the vertical distance of the person, in meters, and $t$ is the amount of minutes since the person started riding.

   (A) Using trigonometric identities, create a rectangular equation that provides the rider's vertical position $y$ and their horizontal position $x$.

   (B) What is greatest horizontal distance between two points on the wheel?

   (C) With respect to the center of the wheel, what is the angular difference between the lowest and highest points on the wheel? Provide your answer in radians.

   (D) A nearby amusement park decides to create a Ferris wheel, where its shape can be defined by the parametric equations $x = 5\cos t$ and $y = 13\sin t$. What is the difference in eccentricity between these two wheels? Include the eccentricity of each wheel in your calculations.

2. The matrices $A$ and $B$ are defined below.

$$A = \begin{bmatrix} 3 & 5 \\ -1 & 1 \end{bmatrix} \quad B = \begin{bmatrix} -2 & 2 & 3 \\ 3 & 5 & -2 \end{bmatrix} \quad C = \begin{bmatrix} 4 & -4 & -6 \\ -6 & -10 & 4 \end{bmatrix} \quad D = \begin{bmatrix} 6 & 3 \\ 2 & 8 \\ 10 & 7 \end{bmatrix}$$

   (A) A fifth matrix, $E$, is defined such that $E = AB$. Find $E$, or indicate that is impossible to find it.

(B) A sixth matrix, $F$, exists such that when multiplied by $A$, it produces the identity matrix. Find $F$.

(C) A student multiplied $C$ by a scalar factor $X$ and produced matrix $B$. Find the matrix produced from multiplying $A$ by this same scalar.

(D) The matrix $D$ was created by multiplying another matrix, $G$, by the determinant of matrix $A$. Find $G$.

# Unit 4 Test Answers and Scoring Guidelines

## Section 1 Answer Key

| 1 | C | 7 | A | 13 | D | 19 | B | 25 | B |
|---|---|---|---|----|---|----|---|----|---|
| 2 | A | 8 | C | 14 | B | 20 | C | 26 | D |
| 3 | D | 9 | D | 15 | D | 21 | A | 27 | C |
| 4 | C | 10 | C | 16 | A | 22 | C | 28 | A |
| 5 | B | 11 | C | 17 | C | 23 | A | 29 | D |
| 6 | D | 12 | B | 18 | B | 24 | D | 30 | C |

## Section 2 Scoring Guidelines

| $t$(s) | 0 | 1 | 2 | 3 | 4 | 5 |
|--------|---|---|---|---|---|---|
| $x(t)$(m/s) | 1 | 4.5 | 17.7 | 73.8 | 313.4 | 1314.0 |
| $y(t)$(m/s) | 0.76 | 2.6 | 8.4 | 27.6 | 91.9 | 307.1 |

The table of above shows the measured velocities of a particle traveling through an inclined particle accelerator. The time, $t$, is measured in seconds. $x(t)$ represents the velocity of the particle in the x-direction while $y(t)$ represents the particles velocity in the y-direction, both of which are measure in meters per second. $\vec{v}(t)$ is a vector-valued function that represents the total velocity of the particle, and $\vec{v}(t) = \langle x(t), y(t) \rangle$.

    A) Find an exponential regression equation for both $x(t)$ and $y(t)$. 2 points

$$\hat{x}(t) = 1.026(4.180)^t$$

$$\hat{y}(t) = 0.769(3.310)^t$$

1 point for the correct $\hat{x}(t)$ equation

1 point for the correct $\hat{y}(t)$ equation

B) Using the regression equations found in part a) find the angle between the two vectors produced at $t = 2$ and $t = 3$. 2 points

$$\vec{v}(t) = \langle 1.026(4.18)^t, 0.769(3.31)^t \rangle$$

$$\vec{v}(2) = \langle 17.922, 8.421 \rangle$$

$$\vec{v}(3) = \langle 74.918, 27.872 \rangle$$

$$\theta = \cos^{-1}\left(\frac{17.922(74.918) + 8.421(27.872)}{\sqrt{(17.922)^2 + (8.421)^2}\sqrt{(74.918)^2 + (27.872)^2}}\right)$$

$$\theta = 0.083$$

Note that using the points in the table given yields $\theta = 0.085$, which is an acceptable answer.

1 point for both correct vectors at $t = 2$ and $t = 3$

1 point for the correct angle

C) State the direction of the particle's velocity at $t = 7$ in both the horizontal and vertical directions. 2 points

1 point for stating that the particle is moving north in the vertical direction.

1 point for stating that the particle is moving east in the horizontal direction.

TOTAL: 6 Points

2. A Ferris Wheel at a new amusement park has an elliptical shape. A person's position on the wheel can be defined by the parametric functions $x = 3\cos t$ and $y = 5\sin t$, where the $xy$ coordinates $(0,0)$ mark the center of the wheel, $x$ is the horizontal distance of the person, in meters, $y$ is the vertical distance of the person, in meters, and $t$ is the amount of minutes since the person started riding

(A) Using trigonometric identities, create a rectangular equation that provides the rider's vertical position $y$ and their horizontal position $x$.

$$x = 3\cos t, \frac{x}{3} = \cos t. \, y = 5\sin t, \frac{y}{5} = \sin t$$

$$\sin^2 t + \cos^2 t = 1, \left(\frac{y}{5}\right)^2 + \left(\frac{x}{3}\right)^2 = 1$$

$$\frac{x^2}{9} + \frac{y^2}{25} = 1$$

1 Point for use of trigonometric identity

1 point for correct answer

(B) What is greatest horizontal distance between two points on the wheel?

Using previous equation, the Ferris Wheel is an ellipse with a horizontal minor axis. $2\sqrt{9} = 6$. The maximum horizontal distance is 6 meters.

1 Point for correct answer with units.

(C) With respect to the center of the wheel, what is the angular difference between the lowest and highest points on the wheel? Provide your answer in radians.

The highest and lowest points of the ellipse lie at the endpoints of the major axis. Because this is a straight line, and the center of the wheel lies on this line, the angular difference between two points on this line with respect to the center must be $\pi$ radians.

1 Point for correct answer in radians.

(D) A nearby amusement park decides to create a Ferris wheel, where its shape can be defined by the parametric equations $x = 5\cos t$ and $y = 13\sin t$. What is the positive difference in eccentricity between these two wheels? Include the eccentricity of each wheel in your calculations. 3 Points.

Eccentricity of first wheel: $e = \dfrac{c}{a} = \dfrac{\sqrt{a^2-b^2}}{a} = \dfrac{\sqrt{25-9}}{5} = \dfrac{4}{5}$

Eccentricity of second wheel: $e = \dfrac{c}{a} = \dfrac{\sqrt{a^2-b^2}}{a} = \dfrac{\sqrt{169-25}}{13} = \dfrac{12}{13}$

Difference in eccentricity: $\dfrac{12}{13} - \dfrac{4}{5} = \dfrac{8}{65}$

1 Point for correct eccentricity of first wheel

1 Point for correct eccentricity of second wheel

1 Point for correct difference in eccentricity

TOTAL: 7 Points

2. The matrices $A$ and $B$ are defined below.

$$A = \begin{bmatrix} 3 & 5 \\ -1 & 1 \end{bmatrix} \quad B = \begin{bmatrix} -2 & 2 & 3 \\ 3 & 5 & -2 \end{bmatrix} \quad C = \begin{bmatrix} 4 & -4 & -6 \\ -6 & -10 & 4 \end{bmatrix} \quad D = \begin{bmatrix} 6 & 3 \\ 2 & 8 \\ 10 & 7 \end{bmatrix}$$

(A) A fifth matrix, $E$, is defined such that $E = AB$. Find $E$, or indicate that is impossible to find it. 1 Point

$$E = AB = \begin{bmatrix} 3 & 5 \\ -1 & 1 \end{bmatrix} \begin{bmatrix} -2 & 2 & 3 \\ 3 & 5 & -2 \end{bmatrix} = \begin{bmatrix} 9 & 31 & -1 \\ 5 & 3 & -5 \end{bmatrix}$$

1 Point for correct answer

(B) A sixth matrix, $F$, exists such that when multiplied by $A$, it produces the identity matrix. Find $F$. 1 Point.

Since the matrices multiply to form the identity matrix, $F$ is the inverse of $A$.

$$inv \begin{bmatrix} a & b \\ c & d \end{bmatrix} = \frac{1}{ad - bc} \begin{bmatrix} d & -b \\ -c & a \end{bmatrix}$$

$$inv\begin{bmatrix} 3 & 5 \\ -1 & 1 \end{bmatrix} = \frac{1}{(3)(1)-(5)(-1)}\begin{bmatrix} 1 & -5 \\ 1 & 3 \end{bmatrix} = \frac{1}{8}\begin{bmatrix} 1 & -5 \\ 1 & 3 \end{bmatrix} = \begin{bmatrix} \frac{1}{8} & -\frac{5}{8} \\ \frac{1}{8} & \frac{3}{8} \end{bmatrix}$$

1 Point for correct answer.

(C) A student multiplied $C$ by a scalar factor $X$ and produced matrix $B$. Find the matrix produced from multiplying $A$ by this same scalar. 2 Points

$$C = \begin{bmatrix} 4 & -4 & -6 \\ -6 & -10 & 4 \end{bmatrix}, B = \begin{bmatrix} -2 & 2 & 3 \\ 3 & 5 & -2 \end{bmatrix}, X = -\frac{2}{4} = -\frac{1}{2}.$$

$$XA = -\frac{1}{2}\begin{bmatrix} 3 & 5 \\ -1 & 1 \end{bmatrix} = \begin{bmatrix} -\frac{3}{2} & -\frac{5}{2} \\ \frac{1}{2} & -\frac{1}{2} \end{bmatrix}$$

1 Point for finding the correct scalar (Note that any division of a value of $B$ by a value of $C$ would suffice).

1 Point for the correct answer.

(D) The matrix $D$ was created by multiplying another matrix, $G$, by the determinant of matrix $A$. Find $G$. 2 Points.

$$detA = \frac{1}{ad-bc} = \frac{1}{(3)(1)-(5)(-1)} = \frac{1}{8}$$

$$\frac{D}{DetA} = 8D = 8\begin{bmatrix} 6 & 3 \\ 2 & 8 \\ 10 & 7 \end{bmatrix} = \begin{bmatrix} 48 & 24 \\ 16 & 64 \\ 80 & 56 \end{bmatrix} = G$$

1 Point for correct determinant of $A$

1 Point for correct answer

TOTAL: 6 Points

# Practice Exam 1

## Section 1, Part A

### Time — 1 hour, 20 minutes

### Number of Questions — 28

A CALCULATOR MAY NOT BE USED ON THIS PART OF THE EXAM.

1. Which of the following is an equivalent form of $16 * 81^x$?

     a. $12^x$

     b. $4 * 9^{2x}$

     c. $16 * 3^{3x}$

     d. $16 * 9^{2x}$

2. Which of the following is an equivalent form of $5 \log x - 12 \log y$, given that $x$ and $y$ are positive constants?

     a. $\log(\frac{5x}{12y})$

     b. $\log(5x - 12y)$

     c. $\log(\frac{x^5}{y^{12}})$

     d. $\log x^5 y^{12}$

3. A polynomial function $f$ is defined $f(t) = (t + 3)(t^2 + 6t + 9)$. Which of the following describes the zeros of $f$?

     a. $f$ has three distinct real zeros.

     b. $f$ has one distinct real zero.

     c. $f$ has one distinct real zero and two non-zeros.

     d. $f$ has three non-real zeros

4. A function $x$ defined $x(a) = \frac{a+3}{a+1}$, while a function $y$ is defined $y(a) = (a^2 + 12a + 4)$. Which of the following gives the composition $x(y(a))$?

     a. $x + 4$

b. $1 + \dfrac{2}{a^2+13a+4}$

c. $1 + \dfrac{2}{a^2+12a+5}$

d. $\dfrac{a^2+12a+6}{a^2+12a+4}$

5. The functions $p$ and $q$ are defined for all real numbers such that $p(x) = q(7x - 21)$. Which of the following are the transformations that map $q$ to $p$ in the $xy$ plane?

    a. A horizontal stretch by a factor of 7 and a shift right by 3 units.

    b. A vertical compression by a factor of 7 and a shift right by 3 units.

    c. A horizontal compression by a factor of 7 and a shift left by 21 units.

    d. A vertical stretch by a factor of 7 and a shift left by 21 units.

6. The function $f$ is defined such that $f(t) = nt^4 - mt^3 + 27$, where $n$ and $m$ are nonzero real constants, and each zero of $f$ is distinct. Given that one root of $f$ is $(3.466, 0)$ and an x-intercept of $f$ is $(a + bi, 0)$, which of the following statements must be true?

    a. $f(t)$ is concave up for all intervals of $t$.

    b. $-3.466$ is a zero of $f$.

    c. $a - bi$ is a zero of $f$.

    d. $f(t)$ has four distinct real solutions.

7. Which of the following gives the fully factored form of $4x^5 - 16x^4 + 20x^3$?

    a. $x^3(x - 2 + i)(x - 2 - i)$

    b. $4x^3(x - 2 + i)(x - 2 - i)$

    c. $4x^3(x + 2 + i)(x + 2 - i)$

    d. $4x^3(x - 2 + i)(x + 2 - i)$

8. Given a piecewise function $f(x) = \begin{cases} 4x + x^2, x \le 2 \\ m^2 - m, x > 2 \end{cases}$, what is the value of $m$ that could make $f(x)$ continuous at $x = 2$?

    a. $m = -2, m = 6$

    b. $m = -6, m = 2$

    c. $m = -3, m = 4$

    d. $m = -4, m = 3$

9. The table below gives the feet of a ball **s** seconds after being shot into the air.

| Time (s) | 0 | 5 | 10 | 15 | 20 | 25 | 30 |
|---|---|---|---|---|---|---|---|
| Height (ft) | 0 | 24 | 52 | 84 | 52 | 24 | 0 |

Which of the following approximates the ball's velocity at $s = 7.5$?

    a. 4.6 ft/s

    b. 2.8 ft/s

    c. 5.6 ft/s

    d. 2.4 ft/s

10. Which of the following is an equivalent expression to $4 \log x^2 - 3 \log 2x - \log x$

    a. $13 \log x$

    b. $15 \log x$

    c. $7 \log x - 3 \log 2x$

    d. $9 \log x + 3 \log 2x$

11. In the Cartesian coordinate plane, what are all the horizontal asymptotes of the graph of $y = \frac{3+4^x}{5-4^x}$?

    a. $y = -1$

    b. $y = 1, y = 4$

    c. $y = \frac{3}{5}$

    d. $y = \frac{3}{5}, y = -1$

12. The polynomial function $f$ is given by $f(x) = 3x^7 - 5x^6 + 41$. Which of the following statements about the end behavior of $f$ is true?

    a. The sign of the leading term is positive, and the exponent of the leading term is odd. Thus, $\lim\limits_{x\to\infty} f(x) = \infty$ and $\lim\limits_{x\to-\infty} f(x) = -\infty$.

    b. The sign of the leading term is positive, and the exponent of the leading term is even. Thus, $\lim\limits_{x\to\infty} f(x) = \infty$ and $\lim\limits_{x\to-\infty} f(x) = \infty$.

    c. The sign of the leading term is negative, and the exponent of the leading term is even. Thus, $\lim\limits_{x\to\infty} f(x) = -\infty$ and $\lim\limits_{x\to-\infty} f(x) = -\infty$.

d. The sign of the leading term is negative, and the exponent of the leading term is odd. Thus, $\lim_{x \to \infty} f(x) = -\infty$ and $\lim_{x \to -\infty} f(x) = \infty$.

13. The graph below displays values of a geometric sequence $a_n$, where the horizontal axis represents values of $n$ and the vertical axis represents values of $a_n$. Which of the following expresses $a_n$ in terms of $n$?

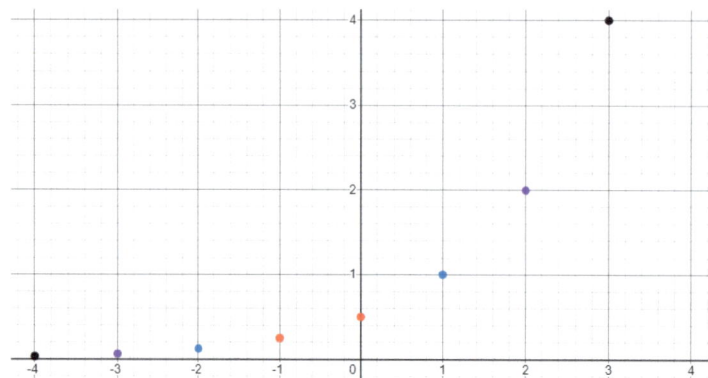

Figure 51 (1). This graph was made on Desmos.com.

a. $a_n = 2\left(\frac{1}{2}\right)^n$

b. $a_n = \left(\frac{1}{2}\right)^n$

c. $a_n = \frac{1}{2}(2)^n$

d. $a_n = (2)^n$

14. Carbon-11 has a half-life of approximately 20 minutes. A lab collected a sample of **150** grams of Carbon-14 and allowed it to decay for **$m$** minutes. Which of the following functions models the remaining amount of grams of Carbon-11, **$g(m)$**, in the sample **$m$** minutes after it started decaying?

a. $g(m) = 150\left(\frac{1}{2}\right)^{\frac{m}{20}}$

b. $g(m) = 150(2)^m$

c. $g(m) = 20\left(\frac{1}{2}\right)^{\frac{m}{20}}$

d. $g(m) = 20(150)^{\frac{m}{20}}$

15. Which of the following functions has a zero at $x = 5$, hole at $x = 4$, and vertical asymptote at $y = 1$?

a. $\dfrac{x^2 - 9x + 20}{x^2 - 5x + 4}$

b. $\dfrac{x^2+9x+20}{x^2-6x+5}$

c. $\dfrac{x^2-2x+1}{x^2-5x+6}$

d. $\dfrac{x^2-6x+9}{x^2-x+20}$

16. Which of the following is equal to $\ln 12 - 6\ln 2 + 2\ln 4$?

    a. $\dfrac{\ln 96}{\ln 4096}$

    b. $\dfrac{\ln 192}{\ln 24}$

    c. $\dfrac{\ln 12}{\ln 8}$

    d. $\ln 3$

17. What are the solutions to $2\cos x = \sqrt{3}$ on the interval $[-\pi, \pi]$?

    a. $\dfrac{\pi}{6}, \dfrac{7\pi}{6}$

    b. $-\dfrac{\pi}{6}, \dfrac{\pi}{6}$

    c. $-\dfrac{\pi}{3}, \dfrac{2\pi}{3}$

    d. $\dfrac{\pi}{6}, \dfrac{5\pi}{6}$

18. The graph below displays the residual plot of a linear function.

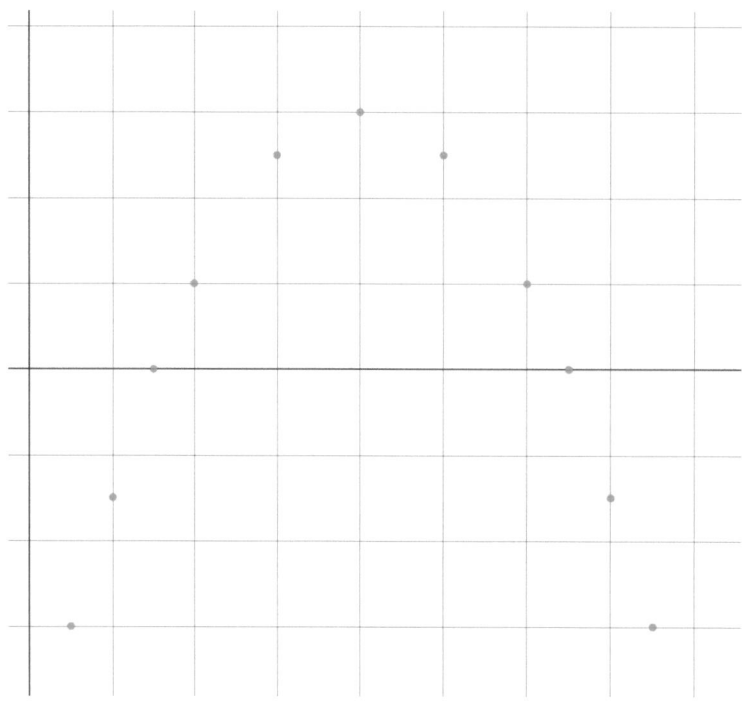

Figure 52 (1). This graph was made on Desmos.com. Assume that the bold horizontal line marks a residual of 0 and serves as the x-axis.

Based on the graph, which of the following is the best interpretation of the plot?

a. There is a pattern in the residuals, and therefore a linear model is valid.

b. There is a pattern in the residuals, and therefore a linear model is invalid.

c. There is no pattern in the residuals, and therefore a linear model is valid.

d. There is no pattern in the residuals, and therefore a linear model is invalid.

19. The table below displays values of $f(x)$ and $g(x)$.

| $x$ | -3 | -2 | -1 | 0 | 1 | 2 | 3 |
|------|-----|-----|-----|-----|-----|-----|-----|
| $f(x)$ | 3 | 6 | 9 | 12 | 15 | 18 | 21 |
| $g(x)$ | 5 | 9 | 13 | 17 | 21 | 25 | 29 |

What is the value of $g(f(-3))$?

a. 3

b. 21

c. 29

d. 17

20. Given that $\log_a 27 = 3$ and $\log_a 12 = 2.262$, find the value of $\log_a 324$?

    a. 1.326

    b. 0.754

    c. 6.786

    d. 5.262

21. Which of the following gives the correct logarithmic equation for the exponential equation $5^x = 625$?

    a. $\log_{625} 5 = x$

    b. $\log_5 x = 625$

    c. $\log_5 625 = x$

    d. $\log_x 5 = 625$

22. James owns a store that sells water bottles. The function that gives the cost, in dollars, of buying x water bottles is known to be $f(x) = 0.50x + 2$, given that x is at least 1. However, on Tuesdays, Mark gives a discount given by the function $d(x) = 0.9x - 1$, where d is the final cost after the discount and x is the cost of the water bottles prior to the discount. Which of the following the gives the function $h(x)$, which gives the total cost of the water bottles after the Tuesday discount in terms of how many water bottles are bought?

    a. $h(x) = 0.45x + 1.8$

    b. $h(x) = 0.5x + 1$

    c. $h(x) = 0.45x + 0.8$

    d. $h(x) = -0.4x + 1$

23. Consider the equation $\tan(\pi + x) + \tan(\pi + x) = 2$. Which of the following values of x satisfies this equation?

    a. $x = \dfrac{\pi}{4}, \dfrac{5\pi}{4}$

    b. $x = \dfrac{3\pi}{4}, \dfrac{5\pi}{4}$

    c. $x = \dfrac{\pi}{4}, \dfrac{3\pi}{4}$

    d. $x = \dfrac{5\pi}{4}, \dfrac{7\pi}{4}$

24. If $\sin x = -\frac{2}{3}$ and $\cos y = \frac{1}{3}$, find $\cos(x + y)$ if $x$ is in Quadrant IV and $y$ is in Quadrant I.

    a. $\frac{\sqrt{3}+2\sqrt{5}}{4}$

    b. $\frac{\sqrt{5}+4\sqrt{2}}{9}$

    c. $\frac{\sqrt{6}+3\sqrt{2}}{16}$

    d. $\frac{2\sqrt{2}+4\sqrt{3}}{6}$

25. The limaçon $r = 3 + 4\sin\theta$ is graphed in the polar plane. Which of the following gives the coordinates of the polar axis intercepts?

    a. $(7, 0)$ and $(7, \pi)$

    b. $\left(7, \frac{\pi}{2}\right)$ and $\left(1, \frac{3\pi}{2}\right)$

    c. $\left(3, \frac{\pi}{2}\right)$ and $\left(3, \frac{3\pi}{2}\right)$

    d. $(3, 0)$ and $(3, \pi)$

26. The rose $r = 17\sin 18\theta$ is graphed in polar plane. Which of the following correctly describes the graph?

    a. The graph has 17 petals, each with a length of 18 units, and the graph is centered on the polar axis.

    b. The graph has 18 petals, each with a length of 17 units, and the graph is centered on the line $\theta = \frac{\pi}{2}$.

    c. The graph has 9 petals, each with a length of 17 units, and the graph is centered on the polar axis.

    d. The graph has 36 petals, each with a length of 17 units, and the graph is centered on the line $\theta = \frac{\pi}{2}$.

27. Solve the following equation on the interval $[0, 2\pi)$: $\cos\left(\frac{\pi}{2} + x\right) - \sin\left(\frac{\pi}{2} + x\right) = 0$.

    a. $x = \frac{3\pi}{4}, \frac{7\pi}{4}$

    b. $x = \frac{\pi}{4}, \frac{5\pi}{4}$

    c. $x = \frac{\pi}{4}, \frac{\pi}{2}$

    d. $x = \frac{5\pi}{4}, \frac{7\pi}{4}$

28. Which of the following is equal to $\tan\left(\theta + \frac{3\pi}{4}\right)$?

    a. $\dfrac{\tan\theta + 1}{\tan\theta - 1}$

    b. $\dfrac{\tan\theta - 1}{\tan\theta + 1}$

    c. $\dfrac{\tan^2\theta + 1}{\tan^2\theta - 1}$

    d. $\dfrac{\tan^2\theta - 1}{\tan^2\theta + 1}$

# Section 1, Part B

## Time — 40 minutes

## Number of Questions — 12

### A GRAPHING CALCULATOR IS ALLOWED FOR THIS SECTION

29. A hose is connected to a tank with a hole on the side. The rate of change of volume of water in the tank is modeled by the function $V$, where $V(t) = 1.280t^2 - 9.857t + 6.346$. $V(t)$ is the rate of change of volume of water in the tank, measured in milliliters per minute, and $t$ is the number of minutes since the tank was opened, where $0 \leq t \leq 10$. At what value of $t$ does the volume of water in the tank change from decreasing to increasing?

   a. $t = 0.709$

   b. $t = 3.850$

   c. $t = 6.346$

   d. $t = 6.992$

30. For the function $K(q) = \dfrac{726}{\log_4 pq}$, where p is a positive constant, $K(7) = 219.511$. What is the value of $K(11)$?

   a. 14.000

   b. 199.813

   c. 239.209

   d. 3.633

31. The population of a town can be modeled by a geometric sequence. In the year 1990, the population was $1,200$ people, and the population in 2000 was $1463$ people. Based on this growth rate, what was the population size in 1995?

   a. 1325

   b. 1332

   c. 1613

   d. 1726

32. The amplitude of a sinusoidal function, $S$, is known to be **3**. Given that a minimum exists at $(\pi, 3)$, which of the following gives a possible equation for $S(x)$?

   a. $3 \sin x + 3$

   b. $3 \cos x + 3$

   c. $3 \cos x + 6$

   d. $3 \sin x + 6$

33. The table below gives values of $g(x)$ for certain values of x.

| x | g(x) |
|---|------|
| 1 | 0 |
| 2 | 1.078 |
| 3 | 1.712 |
| 4 | 2.160 |

Given that $g(x)$ is a logarithmic function in the form $y = \log_a x$, which of the following is a possible value of $g(3.75)$?

   a. 2.059

   b. 1.974

   c. 12.321

   d. 21.090

34. A rose in the polar plane has 12 petals, each with a length of 6 units, and is centered on the polar axis. What are the polar coordinates for the point on the rose with $\theta = \frac{\pi}{6}$?

   a. $(-6, \frac{\pi}{6})$

   b. $(6, \frac{\pi}{6})$

   c. $(-12, \frac{\pi}{6})$

   d. $(12, \frac{\pi}{6})$

35. Consider an arithmetic series where $a_1 = 6$ and $d = 4$. Which of the following represents $S_n$, the sum of the first $n$ terms of the series?

   a. $S_n = 6n + 4$

   b. $S_n = 6n - 4$

c. $S_n = \frac{4n(n+8)}{2}$

d. $S_n = \frac{n(4n+8)}{2}$

36. A population of rabbits is estimated to grow at an exponential rate of approximately 8% every 2 years. After 8 years, which of the following will be true, given that the population size was initially 80?

    a. There will be 112 rabbits.

    b. There will be 106 rabbits.

    c. There will be 109 rabbits.

    d. There will be 144 rabbits.

37. A sequence of numbers is given as 6, 17, 34, 57, ... $n$. Which of the following functions $f(n)$ gives the $n$th term of the sequence?

    a. $f(n) = 3n^2 + 2n + 1$

    b. $f(n) = n^2 + 2n + 3$

    c. $f(n) = 11n - 5$

    d. $f(n) = 17n + 6$

38. Given the equation $f(x) = -0.5x^3 + 6x^2 - 14x + 4$, on which of the following intervals is the function strictly increasing?

    a. $[-1, 0]$

    b. $[0, 1]$

    c. $[1, 2]$

    d. $[2, 3]$

39. What is the value of $3^x$ in the following equation: $7^{2x+1} = 3^{x+3}$?

    a. 0.483

    b. 1.700

    c. 45.915

    d. 61.874

40. What is the value of x in the following equation: $4^{x-3} = 6^{2x-1}$ ?

    a. 1.707

    b. $-1.077$

c. 0.0035

d. 2.585

# Section 2, Part A

## Time — 30 minutes

## Number of Questions — 2

### A GRAPHING CALCULATOR IS ALLOWED FOR THIS SECTION

1. The values of $f(x)$, which is defined for all positive values of x, are shown below. The function $f$ is given by the equation $f(x) = \frac{x}{2} - 3\sqrt{x} + 6$.

| $x$ | 0 | 1 | 4 | 9 | 16 |
|-----|---|---|---|---|----|
| $f(x)$ | 6 | $3\frac{1}{2}$ | 2 | $\frac{3}{2}$ | 2 |

(A) A function $g(x)$ exists such that $f^{-1}(x) = g(x)$. Find the value of $g(16)$. Round your answer to three decimal places.

(B) Determine the end behavior of $g(x)$ as x increases without bound. Express your answer in limit notation.

(C) A translation is performed on $f(x)$ to form $h(x)$, such that $h(x) = f(x - 3)$.

(i) What translation would map $h^{-1}(x)$ to $g(x)$?

(ii) What is the rate of change of $h(x)$ from $x = 3$ to $x = 7$?

2. The pH scale measures the Hydrogen cation concentration of a given substance. It follows a logarithmic scale, where an increase of 1 in the pH value is a ten-fold increase in the hydrogen cation concentration.

(A) Distilled water has a neutral pH, with a pH of 7 and hydrogen cation concentration of $10^{-7}$mol/L. Using this information, calculate the hydrogen cation concentration of lemon juice, which has a pH of 2.

(B) A student is trying to calculate the pH of a substance given hydrogen ion concentration and vice versa.

(i) Write a logarithmic equation that expresses the pH, $P$, of a solution in terms of the hydrogen concentration, $h$

(ii) Write a second equation that expresses the hydrogen concentration, $H$, in terms of the pH, $p$.

(C) Including correct units, calculate the average rate of change of $H$ from $p = 0$ to $p = 3$ and from $p = 4$ to $p = 7$. Which average rate of change is greater? Explain the contextual meaning of this difference.

# Section 2, Part B

## Time — 30 minutes

## Number of Questions — 2

### A CALCULATOR MAY NOT BE USED ON THIS PART OF THE EXAM

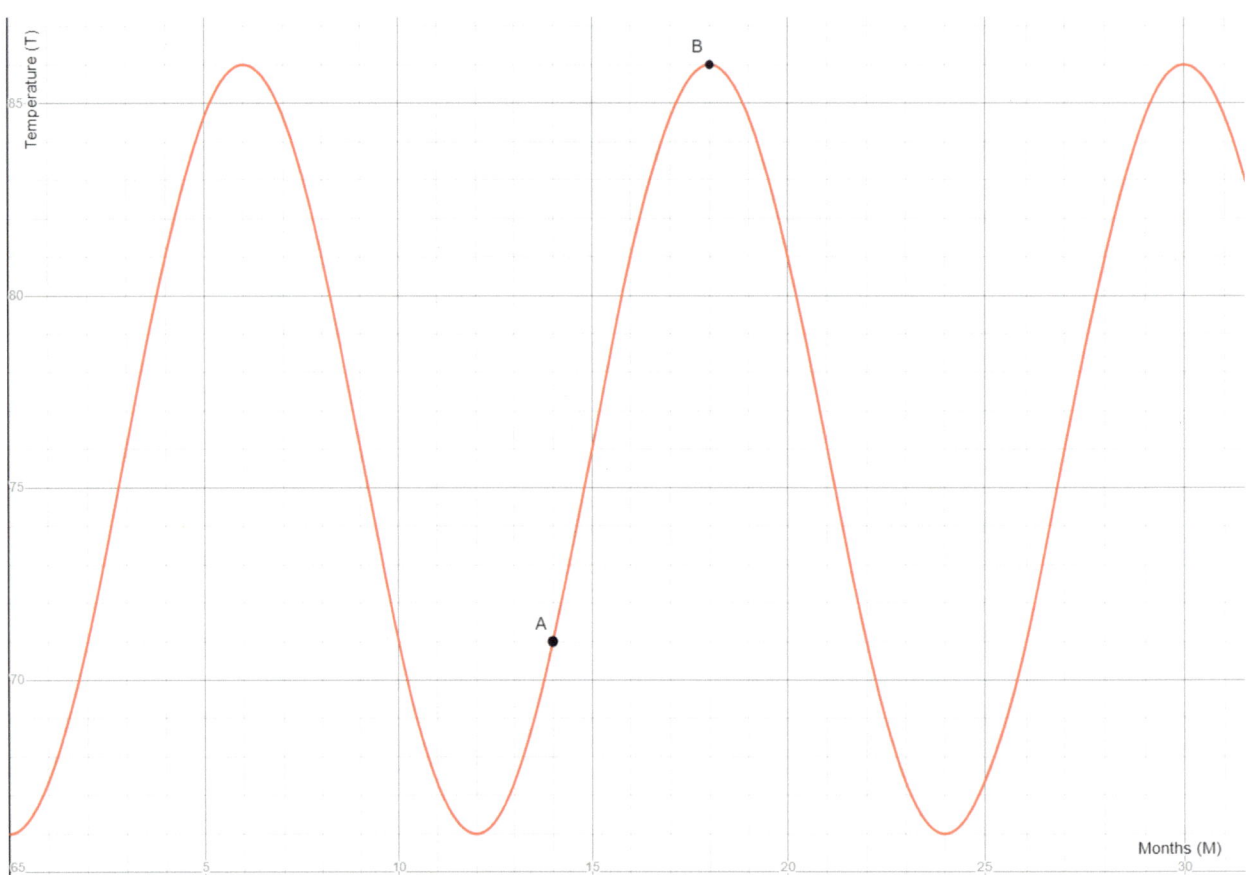

Figure 53 (1). The graph above was made on Desmos.com.

3. The town of Calville has fluctuating temperatures throughout the year. The graph above shows the average high temperature (T) in degrees Fahrenheit of each month (M) in Calville over a 2-and-a-half-year period.

(A) Write a sinusoidal function of the form $T(m) = a\cos(bm + c) + d$ to represent the graph shown in the figure.

(B) (i) Compare the rate of change with the rate of change in the rate of change between points A and B

(ii) Find the rate of change between points A and B

(C) Suppose points C and D were marked on the graph such that C rests on the midline and is between points A and B while D rests on the trough immediately after point B. Approximate the difference, in months and in °F, between the two points.

4. The functions $f$ and $g$ are given by
$$f(x) = 1 - 2\sin^2 x$$
$$g(x) = 4\cos^2 x \tan x$$
(A) (i) Simplify $f \cdot g(x)$ into a trigonometric expression in which only one trigonometric function is involved and appears once.

(ii) Solve the equation $\dfrac{f(x)}{g(x)} = 0$ over the interval $[0, 2\pi)$
$$h(x) = 4\ln x - 1.5\ln x$$

$$j(x) = e^{4x} + e$$

(B) (i) Write a simplified expression for $(h \circ j)(x)$.

(ii) Solve the equation $h(x) = 0$, or indicate that no solution exists.

$$k(x) = 4\tan x \sec x + 5$$

(C) Solve for $k(x) = 5$ over the interval $[0, \frac{\pi}{2})$.

# Practice Exam 1 Answers and Scoring Guidelines

## Section 1 Answer Key

| 1 | D | 9 | C | 17 | B | 25 | D | 33 | A |
|---|---|---|---|----|---|----|---|----|---|
| 2 | C | 10 | C | 18 | B | 26 | D | 34 | A |
| 3 | B | 11 | D | 19 | C | 27 | A | 35 | D |
| 4 | C | 12 | A | 20 | D | 28 | B | 36 | C |
| 5 | A | 13 | C | 21 | C | 29 | B | 37 | A |
| 6 | C | 14 | A | 22 | C | 30 | B | 38 | D |
| 7 | B | 15 | A | 23 | A | 31 | A | 39 | B |
| 8 | C | 16 | D | 24 | B | 32 | C | 40 | B |

## Section 2 Scoring Guidelines

1. The values of $f(x)$, which is defined for all positive values of x, are shown below. The function $f$ is given by the equation $f(x) = \frac{x}{2} - 3\sqrt{x} + 6$. (5 pts)

| $x$ | 0 | 1 | 4 | 9 | 16 |
|-----|---|---|---|---|----|
| $f(x)$ | 6 | $3\frac{1}{2}$ | 2 | $\frac{3}{2}$ | 2 |

(A) A function $g(x)$ exists such that $f^{-1}(x) = g(x)$. Find the value of $g(16)$. Round your answer to three decimal places. (1 pt)

$x = 70.311$

1 point for correct value of $g(16)$

(B) Determine the end behavior of $g(x)$ as x increases without bound. Express your answer in limit notation. (1 pt)

$\lim_{x \to \infty} g(x) = \infty$

1 point for correct limit notation and answer

(C) A translation is performed on $f(x)$ to form $h(x)$, such that $h(x) = f(x - 3)$. (3 pts)

(i) What translation would map $h^{-1}(x)$ to $g(x)$? (1 pt)

A vertical shift 3 units down (1 pt)
1 point for correct translation and magnitude

(ii) What is the rate of change of $h(x)$ from $x = 3$ to $x = 7$? (2 pts)

$\frac{h(7)-h(3)}{7-3}$ (1 pt)

$-\frac{4}{4} = -1$ (1 pt)

The rate of change of $h(x)$ from $x = 3$ to $x = 7$ is $-1$.

1 point for correct formula. 1 point for correct answer.

Total for Question 1: 5 Points

2. The pH scale measures the Hydrogen cation concentration of a given substance. It follows a logarithmic scale, where a decrease of 1 in the pH value is a ten-fold increase in the hydrogen cation concentration. (8 pts)

(A) Distilled water has a neutral pH, with a pH of 7 and hydrogen cation concentration of $10^{-7}$mol/L. Using this information, calculate the hydrogen cation concentration of lemon juice, which has a pH of 2. (2pts)

$7 - 2 = 5. \, 10^{-7} \times 10^5 = 10^{-2}$ mol/L (1 pt)

OR $2 = -\log[H], [H] = 10^{-2}$mol/L (1 pt)

1 point for correct answer, 1 point for correct units. Both methods shown above (multiplying by a power of 10 or using the formula) are acceptable.

(B) A student is trying to calculate the pH of a substance given hydrogen ion concentration and vice versa. (2 pts)

(i) Write a logarithmic equation that expresses the pH, $P$, of a solution in terms of the hydrogen concentration, $h$ (1 pt)

$P(h) = -\log(H)$ (1 pt)

1 point for correct formula and use of variables

(ii) Write a second equation that expresses the hydrogen concentration, $H$, in terms of the pH, $p$. (1 pt)

$H = 10^{-p}$

1 point for correct formula and use of variables

(C) Including correct units, calculate the average rate of change of $H$ from $p = 0$ to $p = 3$ and from $p = 4$ to $p = 7$. Which average rate of change is greater? Explain the contextual meaning of this difference. (4 pts)

$$\frac{H(3)-H(0)}{3-0} = \frac{10^{-3}-10^{0}}{3-0} = -0.333 \text{ (1 pt)}$$

$$\frac{H(7)-H(4)}{7-4} = \frac{10^{-7}-10^{-4}}{7-4} = -0.0000333 \text{ (1 pt)}$$

The average rate of change of $H$ from $p = 0$ to $p = 3$ is greater than the average rate of change from $p = 4$ to $p = 7$. (1 pt)

This means that as the pH values get larger, the difference in hydrogen cation concentration decreases. (1 pt).

1 point for average rate of change from $p = 0$ to $p = 3$. 1 point for average rate of change from $p = 4$ to $p = 7$. 1 point for stating that the rate of change from $p = 0$ to $p = 3$ is higher. 1 point for stating the contextual meaning of the difference.

Total for Question 2: 8 Points

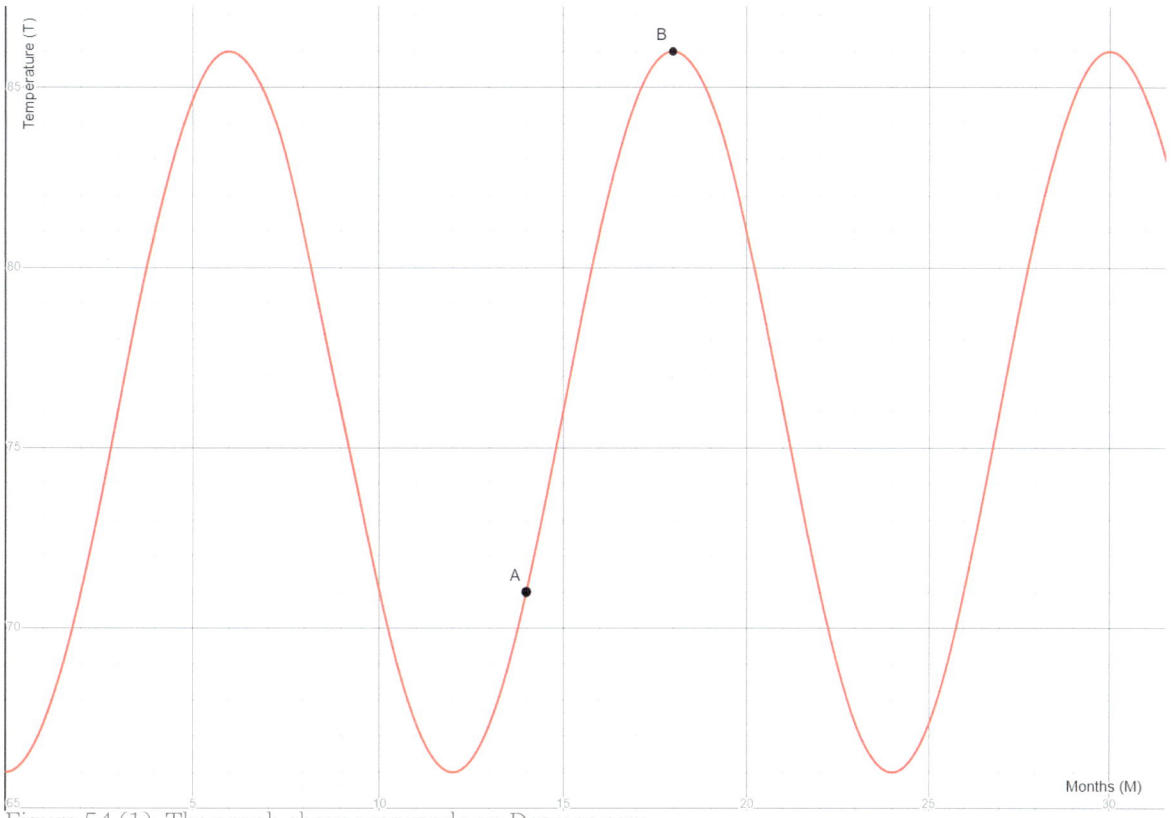

Figure 54 (1). The graph above was made on Desmos.com.

3. The town of Calville has fluctuating temperatures throughout the year. The graph above shows the average high temperature (T) in degrees Fahrenheit of each month (M) in Calville over a 2-and-a-half-year period. (8 pts)

(A) Write a sinusoidal function of the form $T(m) = a\cos(bm + c) + d$ to represent the graph shown in the figure. (1 pt)

$$T(m) = -10\cos\left(\frac{\pi m}{6}\right) + 76$$

$$\text{OR} \quad T(m) = 10\cos\left(\frac{\pi m}{6} - \pi\right) + 76$$

1 point for correct equation with correct variables.

(B) (i) Compare the rate of change with the rate of change in the rate of change between points A and B. (1 pt)

The rate of change between A and B is positive while the rate of change in the rate of change between points A and B is negative. As a result, the rate of change is larger than the rate of change in the rate of change between points A and B.

1 point for identifying the larger rate of change.

(ii) Find the rate of change between points A and B. (2 pts)

$$\frac{T(18)-T(14)}{18-14} = \frac{86-71}{18-14} = \frac{15}{4} = 3.75°\text{F/month}$$

1 point for using the correct formula. 1 point for finding the correct rate of change with units.

(C) Suppose points C and D were marked on the graph such that C rests on the midline and is between points A and B while D rests on the trough immediately after point B. Approximate the difference, in months and in °F, between the two points. (4 pts)

Location of C: $(15, 76)$ (1 pt)

Location of D: $(24, 66)$ (1 pt)

$66 - 76 = -10°\text{F}$ (1 pt)

$24 - 15 = 9$ months (1 pt)

1 point for identifying the location of point C. 1 point for identifying the location of point D.
1 point for identifying the difference in temperature (note that the sign is not necessary to earn the point) with correct units.
1 point for identifying the difference in time with correct units.

Total for Question 3: 8 Points

4. The functions $f$ and $g$ are given by
$$f(x) = 1 - 2\sin^2 x$$
$$g(x) = 4\cos^2 x \tan x$$
(A) (i) Simplify $f \cdot g(x)$ into a trigonometric expression in which only one trigonometric function is involved and appears once. (4 pts)

$f(x) = 1 - 2\sin^2 x = \cos^2 x - \sin^2 x = \cos x \cos x - \sin x \sin x = \cos 2x$ (1pt)

$g(x) = \frac{4\cos^2 x \sin x}{\cos x} = 4\cos x \sin x = 2\sin 2x$ (1 pt)

$f \cdot g(x) = 2\sin 2x \cos 2x = \sin 4x$ (2 pt)

1 point for simplifying $f(x)$. 1 point for simplifying $g(x)$. 1 point for multiplying $f(x)$ with $g(x)$. 1 point for simplifying the product.

(ii) Solve the equation $\frac{f(x)}{g(x)} = 0$ over the interval $[0, 2\pi)$ (2 pts)

$\frac{f(x)}{g(x)} = \frac{1-2\sin^2 x}{4\cos^2 x \tan x} = 0, f(x) = 1 - 2\sin^2 x = \cos 2x = 0$ (1 pt)

$\cos 2x = 0, 2x = \frac{\pi}{2} + \pi n, x = \frac{\pi}{4} + \frac{\pi n}{2} = \frac{\pi}{4}, \frac{3\pi}{4}, \frac{5\pi}{4}, \frac{7\pi}{4}$ (1 pt)

1 point for setting $f(x) = 0$. 1 point for all four values of x. If any value is missing, no point is awarded.

$$h(x) = 4\ln x - \ln x^{3/2}$$

$$j(x) = e^{4x} + e$$

(B) (i) Write a simplified expression for $(j \circ h)(x)$. (1 pt)

$(j \circ h)(x) = e^{4(2.5 \ln x)} + e = e^{10 \ln x} + e = \left(e^{\ln x}\right)^{10} + e = 10 + e$ (1 pt)
1 point for the correct solution.

(ii) Solve the equation $h(x) = 0$, or indicate that no solution exists. (1 pt)
$2.5 \ln x = 0$, $\ln x = 0$, $x = e^0 = 1$

1 point for the correct solution.

$$k(x) = 4\tan x \sec x + 5$$

(C) Solve for $k(x) = 5$ over the interval $[0, \frac{\pi}{2})$. (2 pts)
$k(x) = 4\tan x \sec x + 5 = 5$, $4\tan x \sec x = 0$, $\tan x \sec x = 0$ (1 pt)

$\tan x \sec x = 0$, $\tan x = 0$, $x = 0$; $\sec x = 0$, no solution. Thus, $x = 0$ (1 pt)

1 point for setting $\tan x \sec x = 0$. 1 point for identifying $x = 0$.

Total for Question 4: 10 Points

# Practice Exam 2

## Section 1, Part A

### Time — 1 hour, 20 minutes

### Number of Questions — 28

A CALCULATOR MAY NOT BE USED ON THIS PART OF THE EXAM.

1. Which of the following represents a coterminal angle of $\theta = \frac{13\pi}{4}$ radians

    a. $\frac{17\pi}{4}$

    b. $-\frac{\pi}{4}$

    c. $-\frac{19\pi}{4}$

    d. $\frac{25\pi}{4}$

2. Given that $\log x(4^x) = \frac{x}{6}$, which of the following is the value of x?

    a. $4^6$

    b. $4^{\frac{1}{6}}$

    c. $4^2$

    d. $4^{16}$

3. Which of the following are the factors of the polynomial $f(x) = 4x^8 - 61x^4 + 225$?

    a. $(2x - 5)^2(x - 3)^2$

    b. $(2x^2 - 5)^2(x - 3)^2$

    c. $(2x - 5)(2x + 5)(x - 3)(x + 3)$

    d. $(2x^2 - 5)(2x^2 + 5)(x^2 - 3)(x^2 + 3)$

4. Given that $8^{2x+3} = 2^{9x}$, which of the following is the value of x?

    a. 2

    b. 3

    c. $\frac{1}{3}$

    d. $\frac{1}{2}$

5. Which of the following is equivalent to $\sin^2(\frac{\pi}{3}) + \sec^3(\frac{\pi}{3}) + \cot(\frac{13\pi}{4})$

    a. 8

    b. $\frac{39}{4}$

    c. 9

d. $\frac{37}{4}$

6. Given the polynomial function $f(x) = -7x^7 + 3x^6 + 23x^4 + 13x^3 - 30x + 4$, which of the following statements about its end behavior is true?

    a. The sign of the coefficient of the leading term is negative and the power of the leading term is odd, therefore $\lim_{x\to\infty} f(x) = \infty$ and $\lim_{x\to-\infty} f(x) = 0$

    b. The sign of the coefficient of the leading term is positive and the power of the leading term is odd, therefore $\lim_{x\to\infty} f(x) = \infty$ and $\lim_{x\to-\infty} f(x) = -\infty$

    c. The sign of the coefficient of the leading term is negative and the power of the leading term is even, therefore $\lim_{x\to\infty} f(x) = 0$ and $\lim_{x\to-\infty} f(x) = \infty$

    d. The sign of the coefficient of the leading term is negative and the power of the leading term is odd, therefore $\lim_{x\to\infty} f(x) = -\infty$ and $\lim_{x\to-\infty} f(x) = \infty$

7. Given that $x$, $y$, and $z$ are constants, simplify $2\ln(z) + 5\ln(y) - 15\ln(xy)$

    a. $\ln(\frac{z^2}{x^{15}y^{10}})$

    b. $\ln(\frac{z^2+y^2}{x^{15}y^{15}})$

    c. $\ln(\frac{10z}{15x})$

    d. $\ln(\frac{z^2y^{10}}{x^{15}})$

8. Which of the following is equivalent to $\sin^2(x) - \sec^2(x)\cos^2(x)$?

    a. $\sin^2(x)$

    b. $-\csc^2(x)$

    c. $-\cos^2(x)$

    d. $\cos^2(x)$

9. Which of the following represents the equation $(x-4)^2 + (y+7)^2 = 65$ in polar form?

    a. $r = 14\cos\theta - 8\sin\theta$

    b. $r = 0$

    c. $r = 14\sin\theta - 8\cos\theta$

    d. $r = 8\cos\theta - 14\sin\theta$

10. If $h(x)$ has a slant asymptote of $y = x + 1$, which of the following functions could be equal to $h(x)$?

    a. $\frac{x^2+3x+5}{x+2}$

    b. $\frac{x^3+3x+5}{x+2}$

    c. $\frac{x^2+5}{x}$

    d. $\frac{x^2+3x+5}{x+1}$

11. Which of the following statements describes the zeros of $g(x) = x^3 - 8$?

    a. One real zero and two complex zeros

    b. Three distinct real zeros

    c. Two distinct real zeros and one complex zero

    d. One distinct real zero

12. Given that $m(x) = x^4 - 10x^2 + 9$, which of the following intervals is $m(x) < 0$?

    a. $(-1, 1) \cup (3, \infty)$

    b. $(-\infty, -1] \cup (1, 3]$

    c. $(-3, -1) \cup (1, 3)$
    d. $[-3, 3]$

13. Given that for geometric sequence $\{g_n\}$, $g_1 = 5$ and $g_2 = \frac{5}{2}i$, which of the following is the value of $g_5$?

    a. $\frac{5}{16}i$

    b. $\frac{5}{16}$

    c. $-\frac{5}{16}$

    d. $5$

14. Which of the following is the coordinate of the removable discontinuity of the rational function $\frac{x^3-8}{(x-2)(x+4)}$?

    a. $(-3, 4)$
    b. $(4, -3)$
    c. $(4, 2)$
    d. $(2, 4)$

15. What is the period of function $f(x) = 3\tan(4x - 2\pi) + 7$

    a. $\pi$

    b. $\frac{\pi}{4}$

    c. $\frac{\pi}{2}$

    d. $4\pi$

16. Given that $\cos(\theta) = -\frac{8}{17}$, and $\sin(\theta) > 0$, which of the following is the value of $\cot\theta$?

    a. $-\frac{8}{15}$

    b. $\frac{64}{225}$

    c. $\frac{225}{64}$

    d. $-\frac{15}{8}$

17. Which of the following is equivalent to $\cos(\theta) + \sin(\theta)\tan(\theta)$

    a. $\csc(\theta)$
    b. $\sin(\theta)$
    c. $\sec(\theta)$
    d. $\tan(\theta)$

18. If $f(x) = x^2 - 1$ and $g(x) = \frac{x-1}{x^2}$, which of the following is $g(f(x))$?

    a. $\frac{x^2-2}{x^4-2x^2+1}$

    b. $\frac{x^2-2x+1}{x^4} - 1$

    c. $\frac{x^3-x^2-x-1}{x^2}$

    d. $\frac{x^2}{x^4+2x^2+1}$

19. If $k(x) = (x-1)/(2x-3)$ which of the following is $k^{-1}(3)$?

    a. $-8$

    b. $-\frac{8}{5}$

    c. 8

    d. $\frac{8}{5}$

20. A polynomial function $Q$ is given by $Q(x) = ax^8 - bx^5 + cx^2 + 7$, where $a$, $b$ and $c$ are all real numbers. Each zero has a multiplicity of one, and two of the zeros of $Q(x)$ are $0.048 - 1.36i$, $and$ $9.67 + 0.936i$. Which of the following statements must be true?

    a. The equation $Q(x) = 0$ has 6 real zeros.

    b. $Q(x)$ has two $x$-intercepts.

    c. $Q(x)$ intersects the $x$-axis four times.

    d. $9.67 - 0.936i$ is a zero of $Q(x)$

21. Which of the following is the value of $x$ given that $\ln(x^5) - \ln(x^3) = 3$?

    a. $e^{\frac{3}{2}}$

    b. $e^{\frac{3}{2}}$ and $-e^{\frac{3}{2}}$

    c. $e^{\frac{2}{3}}$ and $-e^{\frac{2}{3}}$

    d. $e^{\frac{2}{3}}$

22. Which of the following are the values of $x$ given that $\log(x) + \log(x + 3) = \log(x + 8)$?

    a. $x = -4$

    b. $x = 2$ and $x = -4$

    c. $x = 2$

    d. $x = -2$

23. What are all the values of $\theta$, for $0 \le \theta \le 2\pi$ for $2\cos^2(\theta) = 3\sin(\theta)$?

    a. $\frac{\pi}{6}$

    b. $\frac{5\pi}{6}$

    c. $\frac{\pi}{3}$

    d. $\frac{\pi}{6}$ and $\frac{5\pi}{6}$

24. Which of the following are the intersection points for $f(x) = 5 + 2\csc^2(x)$ and $g(x) = 13$, for $0 \le x \le \pi$ ?

    a. $\frac{\pi}{6}$ and $\frac{5\pi}{6}$

    b. $\frac{\pi}{6}$

    c. $\frac{5\pi}{6}$

    d. $\frac{7\pi}{6}$

25. The function $h$ is given by $h(x) = 4x^3 - 3x + 7$, which of the following functions is $h(x)$ shifted right 2 units?

    a. $8x^3 - 6x + 14$

    b. $4x^3 - 3x + 9$

    c. $4(x - 2)^3 - 3(x - 2) + 7$

    d. $4(x + 2)^3 - 3(x + 2) + 7$

26. Given the function $f(x) = 4\tan\left(3x + \frac{3\pi}{4}\right) + 7$, which of the following represents the phase shift of $f(x)$?

    a. $\frac{3\pi}{4}$

b. $-\frac{3\pi}{4}$

c. $3\pi$

d. $\frac{\pi}{4}$

27. If $64^x + 64^{-x} = 194$, Which of the following is the value of $8^x + 8^{-x}$?

a. $\sqrt{194}$

b. $64$

c. $14$

d. $8\sqrt{3}$

28. The rational function $h(x)$ has a vertical asymptote at $x = 9$, a hole at $x = 3$, and a horizontal asymptote at $y = 0$. Which of the following could be $h(x)$?

a. $\dfrac{x+7}{x^2-12x+27}$

b. $\dfrac{x^2+4x-21}{x^2-12x+27}$

c. $\dfrac{x^2+4x-21}{x^3-10x^2+3x+54}$

d. $\dfrac{x^2+4x-21}{x^2-7x-18}$

# Section 1, Part B

## Time — 40 minutes

## Number of Questions — 12

## A GRAPHING CALCULATOR IS ALLOWED FOR THIS SECTION

29. Given the function $f(x) = 0.6x^3 + 5.829x^2 + \cos(\frac{\pi}{6}x)$, which of the following is the value of x for which $f(x)$ changes from increasing to decreasing?

    a. $x = 0$

    b. $x = -6.488$

    c. $x = -9.722$

    d. $x = 3.82$

30. If $f(x) = \frac{60}{1+7e^{kx}}$, and $f(3) = 40$, which of the following is the value of k?

    a. $-0.88$

    b. $0.88$

    c. $2.64$

    d. $-2.64$

31. How many times does the function $f(x) = \sin^2(x) + \cos(x) + \ln(x)$ change from increasing to decreasing, for $0 \le x \le 2\pi$?

    a. 4

    b. 5

    c. 3

    d. 2

32. Given the function $f(x) = \sin(x) + \cos(x)$, which of the following specifies a restricted domain for which $f^{-1}(x)$ exists?

    a. $[-\frac{\pi}{4}, \frac{\pi}{4}]$

    b. $[-\frac{\pi}{4}, \frac{3\pi}{4}]$

    c. $[0, \frac{5\pi}{4}]$

d. $[-\frac{3\pi}{4}, \frac{\pi}{4}]$

33. The temperature of a plate after it is pulled out of a microwave is given by the function $T(t) = 175e^{-0.783t}$, where $t$ is the time in seconds. Which of the following describes the behavior of $T(t)$ at $t = 3$?

    a. The temperature is increasing at an increasing rate.

    b. The temperature is increasing at a decreasing rate.

    c. The temperature is decreasing at an increasing rate.

    d. The temperature is decreasing at a decreasing rate.

| $x$ | 1 | 2 | 3 | 4 | 5 |
|---|---|---|---|---|---|
| $f(x)$ | 2 | 14 | 57 | 98 | 174 |

34. The table above shows the values of $f(x)$ at select values of $x$. An exponential regression model, $y = ab^x$ is used to model the data. Which of the following is the predicted value of $f(2.56)$?

    a. 19.139

    b. 19.015

    c. 17.814

    d. 18.809

35. If $f(x) = 3\sin(\frac{\pi}{6}x - 3\pi)$ and $g(x) = (f(x))^2 - 1$, what is the $x$-intercept of $g(x)$ within $0 \le x \le 2$?

    a. $-1$

    b. 0.649

    c. 8

    d. 3

36. Two functions $g(x) = 4\cos(3x + 5\pi)$ and $h(x) = 0.5e^{4.2x}$ are defined in the cartesian coordinate system. At which of the following $x$ values do $g(x)$ and $h(x)$ intersect, for $-1 \le x \le 1$?

    a. $x = -0.528$

    b. $x = 0.513$

    c. $x = -1.047$

d. $x = 0.003$

37. The population of a bacteria colony is modeled by the function $P(t) = \frac{70,000}{1+50e^{-1.5t}}$. If the colony of the bacteria were to exist for an infinite amount of time, what would the population eventually reach?

    a. 50

    b. 0

    c. 70,000

    d. 1

38. Which of the following is the value of $x$ in the equation $2^{3x+7} = 5^{0.5x+4}$?

    a. $x = 0.55$

    b. $x = 5.05$

    c. $x = 0.915$

    d. $x = 1.244$

39. Given the function $f(x) = -0.25x^3 + 2.36x^2 - 2.6x - 8.6$, in which of the following intervals is $f(x) > 0$?

    a. $(-1.367, 3.397)$

    b. $(-\infty, -1.367) \cup (3.397, 7.41)$

    c. $(-1.367, 3.397) \cup (7.41, \infty)$

    d. $(3.397, 7.41)$

40. What is the behavior of the function $h(x) = 3.5 \sin^2(\ln(x + 3))$ at $f(0)$?

    a. Decreasing at an increasing rate.

    b. Increasing at a decreasing rate.

    c. Decreasing at a decreasing rate.

    d. Increasing at an increasing rate.

# Section 2, Part A

## Time — 20 minutes

## Number of Questions — 2

## A GRAPHING CALCULATOR IS ALLOWED FOR THIS SECTION

| $x$ | 1 | 2 | 3 | 4 | 5 |
|---|---|---|---|---|---|
| $f(x)$ | 4 | 9 | 22 | 53 | 122 |

1. The function $f(x)$ is an exponential function. The table gives the values of $f(x)$ for selected values of $x$. A function $g$ is defined by $g(x) = 0.73x^4 - 5.2x^3 + 7$. Round your answers to 3 decimal places.

    a)  i) Find an exponential regression equation for $f(x)$

       ii) Find the value of $g(f(2))$

    b) Describe the left and right end behaviors of $g(x)$

    c) A new function $h(x)$ is defined by $h(x) = \frac{f(x)}{g(x)}$

       i) Find each of the vertical asymptotes of $h(x)$

       ii) As the values of $x$ begin to approach negative infinity what does $h(x)$ approach?

2. A new pesticide is being tested on a population of termites. The population of the termites after the pesticide is administered is defined by an exponential function $P(t) = P_0 e^{rt}$, where $t$ is measured in days. At time $t = 0$ the population of the termites is 700, and at time $t = 3$ the population of the termites is 59.

a) i) Using the data given find the value of $P_0$ and $r$

ii) Using the values of $P_0$ and $r$ from part i) create an expression for $P(t)$

b) i) Using the equation for $P(t)$ found in part a) find the average rate of change of $P(t)$ from $t = 3$ to $t = 3.5$, round to the nearest whole number

ii) Explain your answer from part i) in context of the problem

c) Find the time $t$ needed for the population to half

# Section 2, Part B

## Time — 20 minutes

## Number of Questions — 2

### A CALCULATOR MAY NOT BE USED ON THIS PART OF THE EXAM

3. At a coastal city the height of the tides can be modeled by a sinusoidal function $h(t) = a\sin(bt + c) + d$, where $t$ represents the time in hours, and the height, $h(t)$, is measured in meters. The maximum height of the tide is 3 meters at $t = 12$ hours, and the minimum height of the tide is 1 meter at $t = 4$ hours.

a) The coordinate points $E, F, G, H$, and $I$ exist within one period of $h(t)$. Determine the possible coordinates of these points. Be sure to include the maximum and minimum points provided and use $t = 0$ as the lowest $t$ value.

b) Using the coordinates found in part a) create an expression for $h(t)$.

c) i) Within $0 \leq t \leq 16$ of $h(t)$, on which intervals is $h(t)$ both positive and increasing.

ii) Describe the behavior of $h(t)$ within the interval $4 \leq t \leq 12$

4. A student is studying the properties of various functions

a) The function $h(x)$ and $k(x)$ are given below.

$$h(x) = \frac{x^2}{x^4 + 1}$$

$$k(x) = 2\ln(x)$$

i) Find $k(h(x))$ as an expanded logarithm

ii) Find the vertical asymptotes of $k(h(x))$

b) The functions $f(x)$ and $g(x)$ are given below

$$f(x) = \frac{2\sin(x)\cos(x)}{\cos^2(x) - \sin^2(x)}$$

$$g(x) = 2f(x)$$

i) Simply $f(x)$ to where there is only one trigonometric function

ii) Find the value of $x$ for which $g(x) = 0$ for $0 \leq x \leq \pi$

c) The function $j(x)$ is defined below

$$j(x) = \frac{e^x}{\ln(x)}$$

i) State the positive end behavior of $j(x)$

ii) State the domain of $j(x)$

# Practice Exam 2 Answers and Scoring Guidelines

## Section 1 Answer Key

| 1 | C | 9 | D | 17 | C | 25 | C | 33 | C |
|---|---|---|---|---|---|---|---|---|---|
| 2 | A | 10 | A | 18 | A | 26 | D | 34 | B |
| 3 | D | 11 | A | 19 | D | 27 | C | 35 | B |
| 4 | B | 12 | C | 20 | D | 28 | C | 36 | A |
| 5 | B | 13 | B | 21 | A | 29 | B | 37 | C |
| 6 | D | 14 | D | 22 | B | 30 | A | 38 | D |
| 7 | A | 15 | B | 23 | D | 31 | D | 39 | B |
| 8 | C | 16 | A | 24 | A | 32 | D | 40 | B |

## Section 2 Scoring Guidelines

| $x$ | 1 | 2 | 3 | 4 | 5 |
|---|---|---|---|---|---|
| $f(x)$ | 4 | 9 | 22 | 53 | 122 |

1. The function $f(x)$ is an exponential function. The table gives the values of $f(x)$ for selected values of $x$. A function $g$ is defined by $g(x) = 0.73x^4 - 5.2x^3 + 7$. (6pts)

a) 2pts

i) Find an exponential regression equation for $f(x)$

$\hat{y} = 1.661(2.356)^x$ (1pt)

ii) Find the value of $g(f(2))$

$g(f(2)) = 1005.73$ (1pt)

1 point for the correct regression equation for $f(x)$

1 point for the correct value of $g(f(2))$

b) Describe the left and right end behaviors of $g(x)$(2pts)

$$\lim_{x \to -\infty} g(x) = \infty \text{ (1pt)}$$

$$\lim_{x \to \infty} g(x) = \infty \text{ (1pt)}$$

1 point for correct left end behavior

1 point for correct right end behavior

c) A new function $h(x)$ is defined by $h(x) = \frac{f(x)}{g(x)}$ (2pts)

   i) Find each of the vertical asymptotes of $h(x)$

   $x = 7.096$

   $x = 1.172$

   ii) As the values of $x$ begin to approach negative infinity what does $h(x)$ approach?

   As the values of $x$ approach negative infinity the values of $f(x)$ approach $0$ and the values of $g(x)$ approach infinity.

1 point for both correct vertical asymptotes

1 point for a reasonable justification for why $h(x)$ will approach $0$

2. A new pesticide is being tested on a population of termites. The population of the termites after the pesticide is administered is defined by an exponential function $P(t) = P_0 e^{rt}$, where $t$ is measured in days. At time $t = 0$ the population of the termites is 700, and at time $t = 3$ the population of the termites is 59. (6pts)

   a) 2pts

   i) Using the data given find the value of $P_0$ and $r$

   $P_0 = 700$

   $P(t) = 700e^{rt}$

   $59 = 700e^{3r}$

$$e^{3r} = \frac{59}{700}$$

$$3r = \ln\left(\frac{59}{700}\right)$$

$$r = \frac{\ln\left(\frac{59}{700}\right)}{3}$$

$$r = -0.825$$

ii) Using the values of $P_0$ and $r$ from part i) create an expression for $P(t)$

$$P(t) = 700e^{-0.824t}$$

1 point for the correct values of $P_0$ and $r$

1 point for the correct expression for $P(t)$

b) 2pts

i) Using the equation for $P(t)$ found in part a) find the average rate of change of $P(t)$ from $t = 3$ to $t = 3.5$, round to the nearest whole number

$$\text{AROC} = \frac{700e^{-0.824(3.5)} - 700e^{-0.824(3)}}{3.5 - 3}$$

AROC $= -40$ termites per day

ii) Explain your answer from part i) in context of the problem

Example Response:

"The population of termites is decreasing by approximately 40 termites per day between days 3 and 3.5."

1 point for Correct average rate of change with units

1 point for reasonable explanation of the average rate of change in context of the problem.

c) Find the time $t$ needed for the population to half

$$700e^{-0.824t} = 350$$

$$e^{-0.824t} = \frac{1}{2}$$

$$\ln\left(\frac{1}{2}\right) = -0.824t$$

$$t = \frac{\ln\left(\frac{1}{2}\right)}{-0.824}$$

$$t = 0.841 \text{ days}$$

1 point for showing the correct work to solve for $t$.

1 point for finding the correct value of $t$ with units.

3. At a coastal city the height of the tides can be modeled by a sinusoidal function $h(t) = a\sin(bt + c) + d$, where $t$ represents the time in hours and the height measured in meters. The maximum height of the tide is 3 meters at $t = 12$, and the minimum height of the tides is 1 meter at $t = 4$ hours. (6pts)

a) The coordinate points $E, F, G, H,$ and $I$ exist within one period of $h(t)$. Determine the possible coordinates for each of these points. (2pts)

$E: (4, 1)$

$F: (12, 3)$

$G: (0, 2)$

$H: (8, 2)$

$I: (16, 2)$

Note: The points can be in any order, and the naming of each point is arbitrary.

1 point for the correct values of $t$

1 point for the correct values of $h(t)$

b) Using the coordinates found in part a) create an expression for $h(t)$

max = 3

min = 1

$$d = \frac{\text{max} + \text{min}}{2} = \frac{3+1}{2} = 2$$

$a = max - d = d - min = 3 - 2 = 2 - 1 = 1$

$c = 0$; The period begins at time $t = 0$, therefore $c = 0$

$h(t) = \sin(bt) + 2$

plug in point $H$: $(8, 2)$ from part a)

$2 = \sin(8t) + 2$

$\sin(8b) = 0$

$8b = \pi$

$b = \dfrac{\pi}{8}$

$h(t) = -\sin\left(\dfrac{\pi}{8}t\right) + 2$

OR $h(t) = \sin\left(\dfrac{\pi x}{8} + \pi\right) + 2$

Note: Any of the points found in part a) can be used to find the value of $b$.

1 point for finding the correct values of $a, b, c,$ and $d$

1 point for creating the proper expression for $h(t)$

c) i) Within $0 \leq t \leq 16$ of $h(t)$, on which intervals is $h(t)$ both positive and increasing. (2pts)

$(8, 12)$

1 point for the correct interval

ii) Describe the behavior of $h(t)$ within the interval $4 < t < 12$

Example response:

"Increases at an increasing rate until $t = 8$, after which it increases at a decreasing rate."

1 point for describing the behavior of $h(t)$ within the interval

4. A student is studying the properties of various functions. (6pts)

a) The function $h(x)$ and $k(x)$ are given below. (2pts)

$$h(x) = \frac{x^2}{x^4 + 1}$$

$$k(x) = 2\ln(x)$$

i) Find $k(h(x))$ as an expanded logarithm

$$k(h(x)) = 2\ln(\frac{x^2}{x^4+1})$$

$$k(h(x)) = 2(\ln(x^2) - \ln(x^4 + 1))$$

$$k(h(x)) = 2\ln(x^2) - 2\ln(x^4 + 1)$$

$$k(h(x)) = 4\ln(x) - 2\ln(x^4 + 1)$$

1 point for finding the correct expression for $k(h(x))$ and correctly expanding it.

ii) Find the vertical asymptotes of $k(h(x))$

$$k(h(x)) = 2\ln(\frac{x^2}{x^4+1})$$

$$\frac{x^2}{x^4+1} > 0$$

$$x^4 + 1 > 0$$

$$x^2 = 0$$

$$x = 0$$

Vertical Asymptote: $x = 0$

1 point for finding the correct vertical asymptote.

b) The functions $f(x)$ and $g(x)$ are given below

$$f(x) = \frac{2\sin(x)\cos(x)}{\cos^2(x) - \sin^2(x)}$$

$$g(x) = 2f(x)$$

i) Simply $f(x)$ to where there is only one trigonometric function.

$$f(x) = \frac{2\sin(x)\cos(x)}{\cos^2(x) - \sin^2(x)}$$

$$f(x) = \frac{\sin(2x)}{\cos(2x)}$$

$$f(x) = \tan(2x)$$

1 point for simplifying $f(x)$ into one trigonometric function.

ii) Find the value of $x$ for which $g(x) = 0$ for $0 \leq x \leq \pi$

$$g(x) = 2\tan(2x) = 0$$

$$\tan(2x) = 0$$

$$2x = 0, \pi$$

$$x = 0, \frac{\pi}{2}$$

1 point for finding both values of $x$. Both values must be included to earn the point.

c) The function $j(x)$ is defined below

$$j(x) = \frac{e^x}{\ln(x)}$$

i) State the positive end behavior of $j(x)$

$$\lim_{x \to \infty} j(x) = \infty$$

1 point for both correct left and right end behaviors.

ii) State the domain of $j(x)$

$$\ln(x) \neq 0$$

$$x \neq 0$$

$$\ln(1) = 0$$

$$x \neq 1$$

Domain: $x \in (0, 1) \cup (1, \infty)$

1 point for correct domain.

# Bibliography

Sources below are those used for images/figures. Throughout the book, images are cited as follows: Figure No. (Corresponding Bibliography List No.). For instance, figure 2 (1) means the image is called figure 2 and it is represented by citation 1 in the list below.

1. Desmos.com/calculator
2. Smith, J. (2015, November 30). *Easy way of memorizing values of sine, cosine, and tangent*. Mathematics Stack Exchange. https://math.stackexchange.com/questions/1553990/easy-way-of-memorizing-values-of-sine-cosine-and-tangent
3. *Sinusoidal*. Math.net. (n.d.). https://www.math.net/sinusoidal
4. Libretexts. (2020, July 27). *10.1: Curves defined by parametric equations*. Mathematics LibreTexts. https://math.libretexts.org/Courses/Misericordia_University/MTH_171-172%3A_Calculus_-_Early_Transcendentals_%28Stewart%29/10%3A_Parametric_Equations_And_Polar_Coordinates/10.01%3A_Curves_Defined_by_Parametric_Equations
5. Foundation, C.-12. (2020, May 7). *Conic Sections*. CK12.org. https://www.ck12.org/book/ck-12-algebra-ii-with-trigonometry-concepts/section/10.0/
6. *Vectors components - translational motion - MCAT content*. Jack Weston. (2020, July 20). https://jackwestin.com/resources/mcat-content/translational-motion/vectors-components
7. Chung, F. (2017, October 9). *Vector plot*. GeoGebra. https://www.geogebra.org/m/bAnquQpH

# About The Author

Noel Jeju is currently a Senior at Hebron High School. He has tutored math for hundreds of hours through a variety of both online and in-person services. He loves teaching math and wrote this book in order to help students succeed in the course through spreading his knowledge of Precalculus.

Neil Jeju is currently a Junior at Hebron High School. He has competed and achieved top 3 placements at regional, state, and international math competitions. He loves learning math and wrote this book in order to serve his community through spreading his knowledge of Precalculus.

Made in United States
Troutdale, OR
04/25/2025

30881314R00091